# Getting Started in
# Online
# Investing

## The Getting Started In Series

# Getting Started in
# Online
# Investing

## David L. Brown
## Kassandra Bentley

John Wiley & Sons, Inc.

New York • Chichester • Weinheim • Brisbane • Singapore • Toronto

Published by John Wiley & Sons, Inc.

Published simultaneously in Canada.

This publication is designed to provide accurate and authoritative information in regard to the subject matter covered. It is sold with the understanding that the publisher is not engaged in rendering professional services. If professional advice or other expert assistance is required, the services of a competent professional person should be sought.

Designations used by companies to distinguish their products are often claimed by trademarks. In all instances where the author or publisher is aware of a claim, the product names appear in Initial Capital letters. Readers, however, should contact the appropriate companies for more complete information regarding trademarks and registration.

*Library of Congress Cataloging-in-Publication Data:*
Brown, David L., 1940–
    Getting started in online investing  / David L. Brown and Kassandra
Bentley.
        p.   cm.—(Getting started in series)
    Includes index.
    ISBN 0-471-31703-9 (pbk. : alk. paper)
    1. Investments—Computer network resources.   2. Internet (Computer
network)   3. World Wide Web (Information retrieval system)
    I. Bentley, Kassandra.   II. Title.   III. Series: Getting started in.
    HG4515.95B763   1999
    025.06'3326—dc21                                                   98-51037

Printed in the United States of America

10 9 8 7 6 5 4 3 2

*David Brown dedicates this book to his newest granddaughters*
*Alexandra Michelle Brown and Camden Kae Brown*

*Kassandra Bentley dedicates this book to her mother*
*Effie Lott Wells*

# Contents

# Preface

Since we first wrote about online investing five years ago, the Internet has exploded in a frenzy of growth.

Our first book, *CyberInvesting: Cracking Wall Street with Your Personal Computer*, listed a dozen investing Web sites in a hurriedly written two-page chapter just as the book was going to press (and we had to search hard to find those). In the second edition two years later, we expanded the Internet chapter to a dozen pages and spun it off, so to speak, into its own 350-page book about investing on the Web (*Wall Street City: Your Guide to Investing on the Web*).

As we were writing that book, the commercial Internet was undergoing kaleidoscopic changes and, in the process, transforming virtually every area of our lives—none more so than the way we invest. The average investor now has access to information that once was the province of professional investors. Investing Web sites now number more than 8000. Brokerage commissions for Web-based trades have dropped from hundreds of dollars a trade to as low as $5 per trade. In response, individual investors are logging on to the Internet in unprecedented numbers. More than 14 million are expected to become online investors by 2002.

Sorting through the mind-boggling array of investing information and tools, however, is not an easy task. That's why we wrote this book.

As part of the "Getting Started In" series, this book is aimed at beginning investors. It will help you find and use the vast array of investing resources on the Internet so you can make your own decisions as an investor. We do not, however, tell you how to make money in the stock market or advise you about investing strategies.

So, is this book for you? It is if:

✔ You have an independent, do-it-yourself attitude.
✔ You like the idea of bypassing all the middlemen and digging out the facts for yourself.
✔ You have confidence in your own judgment and decision-making ability.

✔ You have a basic knowledge of stocks and the stock market.

✔ You are familiar with the Internet—or if not, you're learning about it on the side.

✔ You want to become an online investor.

We think you will be surprised, pleased, and perhaps overwhelmed by the quantity and quality of investing information on the Internet. Much of it is free, and even more is likely to become free in the future. One of the trends of investing Web sites is to reduce premiums on information and to move more resources into the free areas of their sites. So, not only is the information out there, much of it is yours for the taking.

Information does not translate directly into talent, wisdom, or skills, but to the extent that information and related tools make for success, the Internet can help you become a successful investor. In this book, we'll introduce you to some of the best investing tools on the World Wide Web.

DAVID L. BROWN
*Houston, Texas*

KASSANDRA BENTLEY
www.cyberinvest.com
*San Diego, California*

*February 1999*

# *Acknowledgments*

We want to thank Dayle Lyons deRaat of San Diego and Kimberly Haley-Coleman of Houston for reading the manuscript and helping us clarify ideas and examples. Dayle is an international travel consultant who has recently ventured into online investing; Kimberly is the senior international market analyst at Wall Street City. The two of them kept us focused on our goal: helping investors, beginning or experienced, get started in online investing. We also want to thank Jonathan Squire of San Francisco, who directed us to many previously undiscovered investing Web sites.

We would also like to thank Mina Samuels and Myles Thompson of John Wiley & Sons, Inc., who invited us to write this book in the "Getting Started In" series, and the millions of investors flocking to the Internet who create the audience for such a book.

As always, we owe a great debt of gratitude to Carolyn Brown and Geri Fries for helping us coordinate schedules, e-mails, and conference calls, this time across two time zones.

# Getting Started in
# Online
# Investing

# Online Investing
## Where the Street Meets the Web

T he lure of online investing is almost irresistible. Just point and click, and you can imagine yourself with double-digit returns, right up there with the likes of Peter Lynch and Warren Buffett.

It's not that simple, of course, but the fact is, the Internet has dissolved the barriers between Wall Street and Main Street and has placed a treasure trove of investing tools within a click of your mouse. More than 8000 investing sites vie for your attention in this *virtual* Wall Street, offering a dazzling array of investing tools: quotes and news, charts and graphs, market stats and commentary; stock searches and screens; stock picks and model portfolios; corporate profiles, earnings estimates, insider trading reports, research reports, 10Ks and 10Qs, economic reports, and much, much more.

To a newcomer, it's a little like standing in a terminal at Kennedy International Airport for the first time, clutching your ticket in one hand and your carry-on bag in the other, listening to a disembodied voice announce flights to Paris, Rome, Geneva, or Athens, and wondering whether you will *ever* find the right gate and the right plane to take you to your desired destination.

Well, cheer up! It's not as bad as all that because you're holding in your hands a virtual tour guide.

To help you get your online bearings, we will start with a walk-through of an investing site with a familiar name. Then we will take you to some of the coolest investing sites on the World Wide Web to show you the full range of tools for each step of the investing process. Along the way, you'll learn the ins and outs of online trading and where to find the best educational tools for investors. You'll also learn about online guides to help you keep up with the ever-changing Web as we move into the next millennium.

So. How *does* one capture the dynamic resources of the Internet in the pages of a book? One way is to describe each of the top investing Web sites. That is where we start, in Chapter 1, but filling an entire book with site tours would be like trying to stuff an octopus into a paper bag, one tentacle at a time.

Another way is to talk about the different kinds of tools, and point out which sites have the best of each. That's more effective, but still a bit unwieldy. For your convenience and ours, we have imposed an artificial structure over the whole thing—sort of like casting a fine net over the octopus—in order to present both tools and Web sites in a logical fashion.

## THE STRUCTURE OF THE BOOK

The structure we've chosen is loosely based on the "cyberinvesting process" that we developed in an earlier book (*CyberInvesting: Cracking Wall Street with Your Personal Computer*, Second Edition, John Wiley & Sons, 1997). The five cyberinvesting steps are:

1. Identify prospects.
2. Analyze prospects.
3. Time each purchase.
4. Monitor your holdings.
5. Time each sale.

This book is not about the investing process itself, however. We do not explain, for example, what makes a stock a potential winner or how to read technical timing signals. These are covered in our earlier book and elsewhere. We simply use the structure—modified somewhat—to present the tools and Web sites for online investing.

Here is the modified structure you'll find in this book, which corresponds roughly to Chapters 2 through 6. In these chapters, we concentrate on stocks. Mutual funds and other investments are covered in later chapters.

### Step 1: Finding Investment Ideas

The first step in any investing strategy is finding the right investment vehicle: a stock, for instance, that has a better than average chance of going up. Such investment ideas are sprinkled like gold dust throughout the Internet. We'll show you where to find:

✔ Stocks of the day (or week or month).

✔ Lists of biggest gainers or most active stocks.

✔ Stocks that made the news.

✔ Stocks that had positive earnings surprises.

✔ Stocks that analysts have upgraded to a "buy."

✔ Stock screens from the experts.

✔ Model portfolios of stocks based on various investing strategies.

✔ Custom search engines that let you search for stocks to match your own wish list.

Many of these investment ideas are free for the taking. The only problem is knowing which is real gold and which is fool's gold. That's where Step 2 comes in.

## Step 2: Evaluating the Stock

Evaluating the underlying strength of a stock is the most important step in the investing process. Does the stock measure up to its good press? What does its history look like? What do the analysts see in its future? Is now the time to buy this particular stock? The answers to these questions can be found on the Web. You can get everything from a brief company overview to an in-depth corporate profile to the voluminous 10Ks and 10Qs that all public companies are required to file with the *Securities and Exchange Commission (SEC)*.

If you know where to find them—and you will when you finish this book—you can also get the scoop on insider trading, earnings estimates from Wall Street analysts, and a company's fundamental and technical profile rendered in cool charts and graphs.

## Step 3: Setting Up and Managing an Online Portfolio

Once you have acquired several stocks, your main concern will be keeping up with them. You'll want to know how each stock is doing and whether there is any reason to sell or perhaps increase your holdings. This was once an arduous task, but it's a snap on the Internet. Free portfolio trackers let you update all your holdings with one mouse click. The best trackers offer alerts that notify you when a stock hits a predetermined high or low or when there is news that might affect the stock. Some even alert you to technical breakouts. We'll show you the ones with the most bells and whistles, as well as some you can download into your favorite money management software.

## Step 4: Keeping Up with the Market

What's the market doing? This is the question of the day (sometimes of the hour) for most investors, and it's answered at seemingly every stop on the Web.

Simple market stats—the daily rise or fall in the Dow, the S&P, and the NASDAQ—are front-page features on most investing Web sites, but these just scratch the surface. On the Internet, you can view the market six ways from Sunday, with charts on dozens of market indexes, three-times-a-day market commentary, and late-breaking market news straight from the news wires. You can learn—as quickly as your broker could in the old days—what the experts think about the latest wiggle in the Dow. We show you where the best original market commentary resides and who offers the most intriguing slants on the market.

## Step 5: Trading on the Web

You can do all these steps without actually placing the buy and sell orders yourself. But why? If you've done all the research and made all the decisions, you're 99 percent there. In Chapter 6 we introduce you to the joys (and pitfalls) of online trading. We talk about security issues and give you some tips to consider before signing up. In Chapter 9 we show how to by-pass the broker altogether and purchase stock directly from the company.

The first six chapters concentrate on stocks, but once you get started in online investing, you may want to expand your horizons. With that in mind, we devote one chapter (Chapter 7) to mutual funds on the Web and another (Chapter 8) to alternative investments, such as bonds, options, futures, and global investing. Then, we introduce you to online communities where you can meet and talk with other investors, and we even say a few words about online banking.

Finally, we talk about online educational resources for the investor, which are of such quantity and quality as to form a virtual university on the Web.

In a sense, our journey into online investing is a little like visiting a foreign country for the first time with someone who has been there before. We'll show you all our favorite sights, uh, sites, and point out others we think you might like to explore on your own. You'll find that we return again and again to a half dozen or so "investing supersites" because, like the Louvre or the Parthenon, they have so much to offer that one visit won't suffice.

In the end, however, this book is just a get-acquainted guide. You'll discover sites and investing tools we have overlooked or that came online long after this book went to press. Because one thing is for certain: The Internet changes continuously. Web sites come and go, and those that remain undergo makeovers with astonishing frequency, introducing new tools and features and, sadly, eliminating some of our favorites. Our only advice is this: Bookmark your favorite sites for a return visit and check out each Web site's financial links. You never know what treasures may be waiting at the next jump.

Before we begin our journey in earnest, let's acclimate ourselves with a short walking tour of the finance section of the most popular Web site in cyberspace: Yahoo!

Terms appearing in the text in italics are defined in the Glossary beginning on page 229.

*Chapter*

# 1

# Easing In
## A Quick Tour of Yahoo! Finance

Yahoo! is the Grand Central Station of the Internet. It is the best known of the Internet *search engines*, with millions of visitors each day. We're going to bypass the main site, however, and go directly to the finance section, which is called Yahoo! Finance. Here you'll find a sampling of the tools (though not the fanciest ones) needed by the online investor. It's a good place to get your online investing legs.

Figure 1.1 shows the home page of Yahoo! Finance (www.quote. yahoo.com). The most basic elements of investing are here: a quote retriever and portfolio tracker, as well as market stats and news.

## GET A QUOTE

Every investing site worth its *URL (Uniform Resource Locator)* offers free stock quotes. It's sort of like the complimentary bread and water offered by restaurants—it's a way of saying "welcome" and "please come back." For the most part, the quotes are *delayed quotes*—delayed 15 or 20 minutes by the stock exchanges—although more and more sites are beginning to offer free *real-time quotes*.

To retrieve a quote online, type a ticker symbol in the quote box and press Enter or click the Get Quotes (or Go or Submit) button. To retrieve multiple quotes at Yahoo!, enter multiple symbols separated by a space or comma. (Some sites allow multiple quote retrieval only

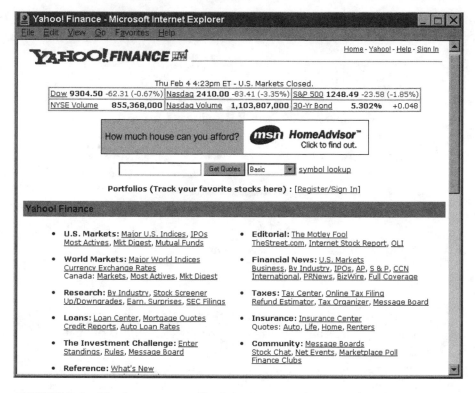

**FIGURE 1.1** The home page of Yahoo! Finance. (Reprinted with permission of Yahoo!)

**Real-Time Quotes**   Stock quotes that include the most recent trade, as opposed to quotes that are delayed 15 or 20 minutes by the exchanges. Real-time, continuous live quotes, offered by some Web sites, are real-time quotes that are automatically updated with each new tick of the stock.

**Symbol Lookup**   If you don't know the stock symbol, use the site's symbol lookup feature. It is better to enter a partial company name unless you know the exact name of the company. You'll get a list of all possible matches.

through a portfolio.) Figure 1.2 shows Yahoo! Finance's basic quote table for three stocks.

✔ Basic performance data is included with the quotes: the last trade, the percentage *and* point change from the opening trade, and the volume. *Hyperlinks* in the More Info column will lead you to research tools for each stock. Recent news headlines appear below the quote table. The quotes can be *downloaded* into a spreadsheet by clicking Download Spreadsheet Format.

✔ Click on the stock symbol for a more detailed view of performance and fundamental information. On that view, click the tiny one-year chart to enlarge it to full size.

If you tire of entering symbols each time you want quotes on your favorite stocks, you can use one of the many *portfolio trackers* on the Web.

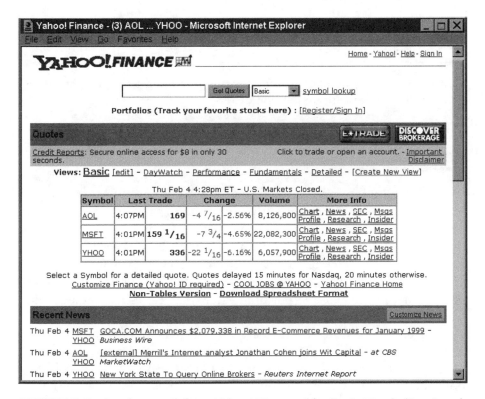

**FIGURE 1.2** Stock quotes from Yahoo! Finance (the Basic View). (Reprinted with permission of Yahoo!)

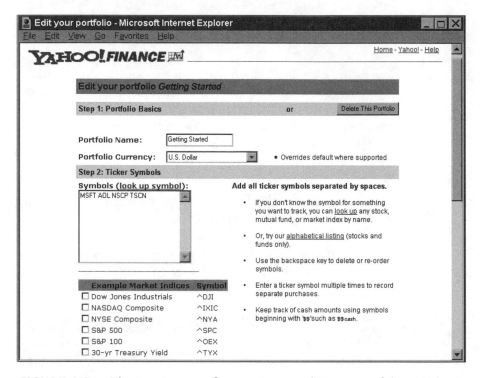

**FIGURE 1.3a** The input screen for creating or editing a portfolio at Yahoo! Finance. (Reprinted with permission of Yahoo!)

## PORTFOLIOS

Free portfolio trackers are used as carrots by Web sites to get your return business. They are among the truly useful freebies to come out of the intense competition among investing Web sites. A portfolio tracker retains the ticker symbols you enter so that you can retrieve quotes for the entire portfolio with one click of your mouse. Most trackers let you enter details of each trade (price paid, commission, number of shares) so that you can track your wins, losses, and portfolio value. Many sites let you keep multiple portfolios, each tracking from 10 to 100 stocks.

Figures 1.3a, 1.3b, and 1.3c show the screens for creating a portfolio at Yahoo! Finance.

The setup process couldn't be more simple: Enter a name for the portfolio; enter the ticker symbols of your holdings; check the market indexes you want to include, if any; select the basic display features, including the default view (the one you wish to see each time you log on); and

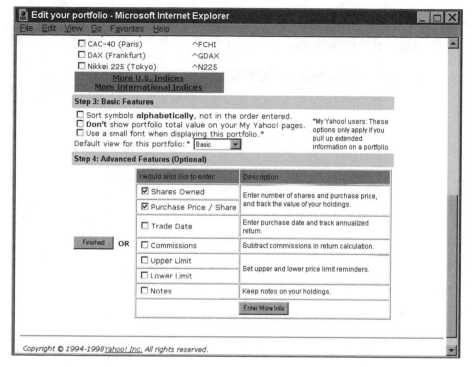

**FIGURE 1.3b** Continuation of the Yahoo! portfolio tracker input screen. (Reprinted with permission of Yahoo!)

click Finished. If you want to track additional information, such as number of shares, purchase data, price alerts, or notes about a trade, click the related boxes, then click Enter More Info to finish. You'll see the screen shown in Figure 1.3c, where you can enter the optional information for each holding. Voilà! You have an online portfolio.

At Yahoo!, the portfolio screen is virtually identical to the quotes screen. The main difference will be found in the Performance View (Figure 1.4), which shows the portfolio's value and gain or loss.

Like the Quotes screen, the More Info column for each stock has links to research information about the stock. Let's look more closely at these links:

✔ <u>Chart</u> displays a one-year chart for the stock. The time frame can be changed to one day, five days, three months, two years, five years, or maximum data. You can also compare the stock to the S&P 500, or plot the 50-day and 200-day *moving averages*.

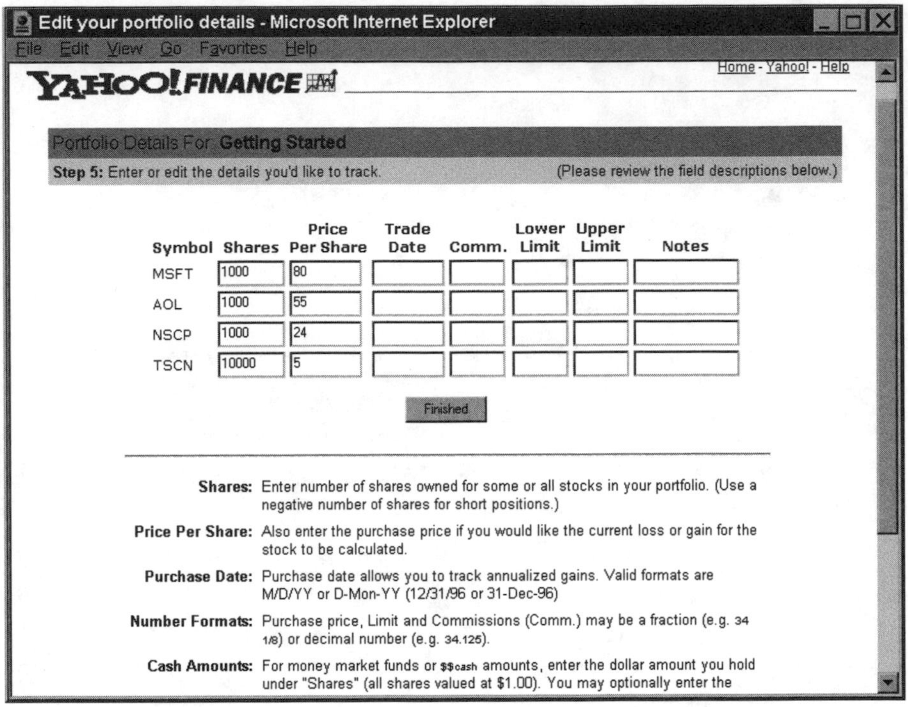

**FIGURE 1.3c**   The final screen in the portfolio tracker setup. (Reprinted with permission of Yahoo!)

✔ <u>News</u> displays news headlines for the stock for the past several months. Click the headline to go to the article.

✔ <u>SEC</u> links to the Management's Discussion from the latest 10Q or 10K.

✔ <u>Msgs</u> takes you to a Yahoo! message board about the displayed stock. We talk about message boards and chat rooms at length in Chapter 9. Be sure to read the caveats in that section.

✔ <u>Profile</u> links to a brief overview of the company.

✔ <u>Research</u> links to a page that tallies the buy/hold/sell recommendations from the analysts, along with a brief look at earnings projections.

✔ <u>Insider</u> links to a listing of the most recent buys and sells of the company stock by corporate insiders.

All this . . . and we're just at the getting-to-know-you stage in online investing!

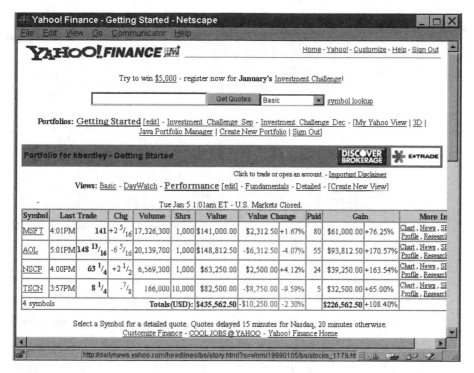

**FIGURE 1.4** The Performance View of a portfolio at Yahoo! Finance. (Reprinted with permission of Yahoo!)

## MARKET NEWS AND UPDATES

Yahoo! Finance has a great deal of market data and financial news, but it is all fairly cut-and-dried. You'll find *market stats* for the Dow, NASDAQ, and the S&P 500 at the top of the home page, plus the trading volume for the NASDAQ and the New York Stock Exchange and the *yield* for the 30-year bond (see Figure 1.1). Click the index name for a detailed view and a one-year historical chart.

**Delayed versus Real-Time Market Updates** Like stock quotes, market stats are also delayed 15 to 20 minutes by the stock exchanges. However, many sites refresh market stats every five minutes or so.

**Registration Required**  Many Web sites require that you register before you can enter the site; some require registration before they'll let you use certain features, such as a portfolio. In most cases, the registration form is simple and requires your e-mail address and a user name and password (which you select). Some sites, however, require that you complete a short demographic survey which will be used for marketing the site. Most sites offer assurance that they won't sell the information to others. Registration is part of the Internet experience. If you want to sample the best investing tools the Web has to offer, you'll have to play the registration game. Our advice: Use the same user name and password for as many sites as possible. Different formats won't allow you to be totally consistent, though, so keep a reference list near your computer.

Links to market updates for other U.S. and world markets appear below the title bar in the middle of the page. The news of interest to investors is under the Research heading (*earnings surprises, upgrades/downgrades, SEC filings*) and the Financial News heading. The Latest Market News at the bottom of the page has a digest of articles from the front page of the *New York Times*.

**Upgrades/Downgrades**  Analysts make buy/hold/sell recommendations for the stocks they follow. An upgrade is a change from a sell to a hold or buy, or from a hold to a buy. A downgrade is a change from a buy to a hold or sell, or from a hold to a sell.

As an investing site, Yahoo! Finance is a good search engine. That is to say, it has a lot of information, but it is not our site of choice for monitoring the market. There are many more sophisticated ways to follow and analyze the market, and we'll look at several in Chapter 5.

## SUMMARY

Our tour of Yahoo! Finance has barely scratched the surface of online investing. We have dozens of stops before we finish our journey, some of which we'll return to again and again as we work our way through the steps of the investing process. Just keep in mind, this is a get-acquainted tour. All we can do is hit the high spots and leave the rest to your future exploration. With that in mind, you might wish to *bookmark* your favorite sites as we go along so that you can return to them with ease.

# Finding
# Investment Ideas
## Lists & Picks &
## Searches & Screens

I dentifying investment opportunities is the first step in any investing strategy. As recently as 10 years ago, nonprofessional investors had to rely on tips from brokers or friends or depend on their own acuity to sniff out the next Microsoft by reading newspapers and periodicals. Now all you need to do to find investment ideas is surf the World Wide Web.

In our *CyberInvesting* book, we call this step of the investing process "stock prospecting," because, like the gold prospectors of the Old West, we may dream of the mother lode that will make us rich, but we'll pan for gold in any old stream. What we're looking for are stocks with the best potential for price increase. This is an obvious first step in the investing process. But until the coming of the World Wide Web, it was not a particularly easy one. Now there's a cyber-universe brimming with investment ideas and online tools that let you point and click your way to a short list of potential winners.

There are so many ideas, in fact, that you have to pick and choose very carefully. When possible, you should prequalify a stock by using the resources that reflect your investing philosophy or style. If you're new to investing, however, you may not yet have a well-defined investing style. To show you the possibilities, let's take a brief look at investing styles before we examine the tools themselves.

## INVESTING STYLES

Investing style has to do with risk tolerance, reward goals, and time horizon. How much risk are you willing to take? Can you watch the ups and downs of the market without breaking into a cold sweat? Or do you panic at the first dip in the Dow? Do you like the security of the *blue chips*? Or the excitement of the more volatile *high techs*? How big a reward do you want and how quickly do you want it? Are you looking for slow, steady growth or quick, smaller profits? The answers to these questions will help you determine your compatibility with different investing styles.

**Mid- to Long-Term Investors**    In general, short-term investors hold stocks less than three months. Long-term investors usually hold stocks more than a year. In between are the mid-term investors, who hold stocks from three months to a year.

The major investing styles are growth, value, fundamental, and momentum. Minor styles have developed around *emerging growth stock* investors, technicians, traders, short sellers, and IPO investors. Books have been written about all of these, so we'll only skim the surface here and point out the characteristics of each style. Keep in mind that investing styles can overlap; we are making clear-cut distinctions for explanatory purposes.

### *Growth Investors*

Growth investors look for stocks with a strong earnings trend and earnings history, usually in growth industries, and they're willing to pay the often high prices associated with growth stocks. They are mid-term to long-term investors who have the patience to wait for the next quarter's earnings release, and possibly sit through many quarters. The growth investor needs a strong enough stomach to endure the occasional disappointing quarter.

**No. 1 Growth Investor**    Peter Lynch used growth investing to rack up high returns for Fidelity Magellan Fund.

### Value Investors

Value investors are the perennial bargain hunters who don't like risk. The essence of value investing is to purchase stocks that are depressed in value and have little further downside, *but* at the same time have considerable potential for appreciation. These are companies with intrinsic value: stocks with good earnings potential and low *price-to-earnings ratios* (*P/E ratios*) as compared with peer companies. The value investor believes such companies to be extremely undervalued. Thus, value stocks theoretically involve less downside and thus less risk. The catch? Value investors need the patience to hold their positions for one to several years to get the return they want.

**No. 1 Value Investor**   Warren Buffett helped popularize value investing.

### Fundamental Investors

Fundamental investors walk like a value duck and talk like a value duck, but they're a slightly different bird. Instead of looking for undervalued earnings, they eyeball a company's balance sheet for undervalued assets: low debt, low *price-to-book ratio*, and high *cash flow*, all at a cheap price. The fundamental investor needs even more patience than his or her value counterpart because it may take longer for the market to recognize the value of the undervalued assets and do something about it. It may take years for the payoff, but such assets are not likely to decline in value, so there is generally much less risk.

**Price-to-Book Ratio**   A company's stock price divided by its book value.

**Cash Flow**   A company's net income with adjustments for noncash items. For example, a noncash expense such as depreciation would be added back to net income to arrive at cash flow.

**No. 1 Fundamentalist** The legendary Benjamin Graham was the original fundamental investor.

## Momentum Investors

Momentum investors are the high rollers. They'll buy a stock at its all-time high without blinking, if it got there on strong *momentum*. These are high-risk, quick-reward kinds of guys who could care less about the name of the stock, much less its *fundamentals*. They look for stocks in a strong upward trend with increasing volume, and they want similar movement in the industry group. Their motto: Get in on the upswing; then take your profits and run.

**No. 1 Momentum Player** The leading proponent of momentum investing is William O'Neil, publisher of *Investor's Business Daily*.

## Emerging Growth Investors

Emerging growth investors are looking for the next Yahoo! or Amazon.com. They're willing to bet on fledgling companies with little or no revenues and usually no earnings (often large losses) in upstart industries with (often) unproven technologies. These are the visionaries who bought biotech stocks in the early 1980s and are buying Internet stocks in the late 1990s. They are expecting *ten-baggers* or better. It's a high-risk kind of investing, but most extraordinary investing stories—such as a stock like eBay or uBid doubling and tripling in one day—come from this area.

**Ten-Bagger** A stock that has a tenfold increase in price.

## Technicians

Technicians have a lot in common with momentum investors. They deal strictly with charts and graphs, putting all their faith in patterns and trends. But they are not necessarily momentum addicts. There are dozens of technical strategies a technician might follow, each with its own guru and disciples. Gerald Appel, for example, with his *moving average convergence/divergence (MACD)* theory; John Bollinger with his well-known *Bollinger bands*. Technical trading is usually short-term and inherently involves a bit more risk due to the lack of concentration on fundamentals.

**Moving Average Convergence/Divergence (MACD)**
A trading method based on the crossing of two exponential moving averages above and below a zero line. (A third moving average plots the difference between the other two and forms a signal line.) The convergence and divergence of the moving averages generate buy and sell signals.

**Bollinger Bands**   A variation on trading bands created by John Bollinger, in which the envelope is plotted at standard deviation levels above and below the moving average, which allows the bands to self-adjust to the volatility of the market (they widen during periods of volatility and contract during periods of calm).

## Traders

There are investors and then there are traders. Investors are the more contemplative sort, carefully researching and evaluating a stock, whether for the short or the long term. Traders, on the other hand, are always short-term, concentrating on patterns and trends, just like technicians. (All traders are technicians but not all technicians are traders!) Traders will trade any security that offers a quick turnaround: stocks, options, futures. This kind of trading involves relatively high risk, again because of the implied lack of concentration on fundamentals (although technicians would argue this point).

*Day trading* is the practice of basing trades on daily market fluctuations and closing out positions by the end of the trading day. Mark A. Seleznov, managing partner of Trend Trader (www.trendtrader.com) calls the electronic day trader the "gunslinger of equity trading" and suggests that day traders need training, dedication, discipline, and at least $100,000 in trading capital.

### Short Sellers

Most investors hope their stocks will go up. Short sellers hope theirs will go down. They sell stocks they believe are overvalued (stocks they don't own which they borrow from brokerage houses) or stocks that are in a downtrend, with the intention of buying them back at a lower price (called "covering a position"). *Short selling* involves high risk because of the unlimited potential for loss and limited potential for reward. For example, if you short sell a stock for $10,000, the most you can make on that stock is the $10,000 you received (if the stock goes to zero and you don't have to cover). However, if the stock goes up, your potential for loss is unlimited because you have to cover your position at the higher price. Often the very pressure of short sellers covering their positions pushes the stock price higher and higher.

 **Covering a Position**    Buying shares in the open market to pay back the shares borrowed when selling short.

### The IPO Investor

Investing in *initial public offerings (IPOs)* is not exactly a style of investing, but it is unique enough to be included here as a subset of investing styles. IPOs involve fairly high risk because of their often scant operating history. Despite the highly publicized IPOs of Internet stocks, it is more common for a stock price to drop, rather than rise, after the initial offering. Too, the hot issues—the ones that stand the most chance of skyrocketing—are usually so overbought that the average investor has little chance of buying shares at the *offering price*. We'll talk more about IPOs and their online counterpart, the *direct public offering (DPO)*, in Chapter 9.

We will explore the tools that go with these investing styles as we discuss the online investment ideas in this chapter. But before we go any further, let's examine the types of prospecting tools you'll find on the Web.

## ONLINE PROSPECTING TOOLS

Repeat traffic is the currency of the Web. Each time you return to a Web site, your visit to the home page counts as a *page impression* for that site. Each click to a different page within the site counts for still another page impression. It all adds up to marketable currency for the site in the form of advertising revenues.

One way that a Web site generates traffic is to offer free features of value that change frequently. Many sites use such features as stock picks, hot stock lists, model portfolios, stock searches and screens, stocks in the news, and chat rooms to keep us coming back for more. These are usually free and present useful sources of investment ideas.

## Picks and Portfolios

On some Web sites a stock pick is the winning entry in an ongoing beauty contest. A resident expert picks a stock based on his or her investing strategy and proclaims it as the "stock of the day" or "stock of the week." Usually, the experts present a detailed analysis of the stock to justify their choice, which gives you a glimpse into the mind of a professional stock picker. This makes for an excellent learning tool, as well as a good prospecting tool, but you will want to look for stock picks that match your investing style.

A variation on the stock pick is the model portfolio. Stocks in a model portfolio are selected on the basis of a particular strategy and followed over a period of time. Buy, hold, or sell recommendations are given regularly for each stock. The "buys" are a good source for investment ideas.

Stock picks and model portfolios—like all investment ideas—are just that: ideas. Never accept any of them on faith. Check out the expert's reasoning; then do your homework online, as we explain in the next chapter.

## Hot Stock Lists

Hot stock lists are a staple on investing Web sites. These lists present stocks that have been identified or screened for certain characteristics. Some lists contain the day's most active stocks—stocks with the biggest percentage gain or highest volume. Others offer a basket of stocks chosen for a particular trait or group of traits.

Lists are good prospecting tools if the underlying strategy matches your own. For example, a "big movers" list could be a good source for a momentum investor. A basket of stocks based on high earnings estimates could aim a growth investor in the right direction.

If you use lists as a source of investment ideas, skim off the top 10 or 20 stocks to make your own short list and then, again, *do your homework.* (We'll show you how in the next chapter.)

### Searches and Screens

A stock search or *screen* can turn up a powerful list of potential winners. It is one of the best prospecting tools because the screen can be chosen to reflect your unique objectives, biases, and investing style.

There are two kinds of searches and screens: preset and custom.

**Preset Screens**  A preset screen is like the membership committee at an elite social club. This powerful group lays down the rules for membership and allows only those who meet strict standards to join the club. Likewise, certain value and performance *criteria* act as standards for admittance in a preset stock screen: All the stocks in a database are run through the screen and only those that meet the standards are accepted as prospects.

The name given to a preset screen—undervalued growth stocks, contrarian screen, basing pattern breakouts—reveals (or should reveal) its underlying strategy. Usually, a description of the strategy is linked to the name of the screen, along with a list of criteria used in the screen. (The best screens also link to criteria definitions.)

A few preset screens are prerun. This means the Web site presents a list of stocks from a screen that was run on a particular day or week. The best screens are those that can be run on current market data.

**Custom Searches and Screens**  If you want to set your own standards by which stocks are judged, look for a custom search or screen. These allow you to select your own criteria and enter the values for each. You can, for example, specify that historical earnings be "as high (or low) as possible" or enter minimum or maximum ranges. In the best searches, you can also require that an indicator (stock price, for example) be displayed only and not affect the search.

There are three things to look for when using custom searches and screens:

1. The number and type of criteria available for designing a search.
2. The degree of user input allowed.
3. The ease of designing the search.

The criteria for custom searches range from 20 or so to over 700, and user input varies widely. Probably most important is the ease of designing a search, because if you fail in that, your search results may be meaningless.

Look for searches that offer menu selections for criteria, easy links to definitions, variables that make sense, and a help section that offers step-by-step instructions for designing the search. We'll point out these features when we discuss the specific tools later in the chapter.

## Stocks in the News

News can be a good source of investment ideas, but with the flood of news on the Internet, the problem is too much of a good thing. The solution is to look for categorized news.

Two of the best categories for investment ideas are *research alerts* and upgrades/downgrades. Research alerts are revisions in the analysts' earnings estimates for a stock. Upgrades/downgrades are changes in an analyst's buy/sell/hold recommendations. Look for investment ideas in stocks with upward revisions or stocks that have been upgraded from a sell or hold to a buy. (Short sellers would look for downgrades to a sell or downward revisions in estimates.)

 **Finding Research Alerts** Three sites reporting research alerts and upgrades/downgrades are MSN Investor, Quicken.com, and StockSite.

Keep in mind that these are categories used by Web sites, and the categories sometimes overlap. Upgrades and downgrades often involve a revision in earnings estimates, and revised estimates may result in an upgraded or downgraded recommendation.

Stocks that make news for other reasons, such as new product announcements or clearance by some governmental regulatory agency, may also be a source of investment ideas, but keep this in mind: By the time the mass media reports it, chances are the news will have already been reflected in the stock price (because of rumors on Wall Street that precede the story). How to tell? If the stock has recently made a sharp move, you can assume the news was out before it hit the press. There may still be some fizz left, but such stocks should be evaluated with a skeptic's eye.

## Chat Rooms/Message Boards

The Internet is a collection of communities, and interaction with similarly feathered birds is part of its lure. That explains the ubiquity of *chat rooms* and *message boards*. They are just one more frequent-visitor carrot in a site's traffic-building salad.

> **Internet Scams**    Stocks praised or bashed in chat rooms and on message boards should be treated with a healthy dose of skepticism. But these are not the only media for scams. Unsolicited e-mails that promote obscure stocks should also be greeted with caution, especially if huge gains are promised or implied. To file a complaint, e-mail the Securities and Exchange Commission at help@sec.gov or call them at 202-942-7040.

These cyber-watering holes are not the best prospecting tools. In fact, in our opinion, they are lousy. You'll find highly touted stocks amid the chatter, but you don't have a clue as to the expertise, experience, or agenda of the person touting a stock. In Chapter 9, we'll tell you where to find the most active rooms and boards, but our strong advice is: Chatter, beware! Because of their unregulated nature, chat rooms and message boards are hotbeds for con games and scams. If something sounds too good to be true, it probably is.

On the other hand, beware of someone whipping a stock with an oversized stick. Those who berate a stock loudest and longest are quite possibly short sellers caught in a squeeze trying to beat down the stock price.

## THE TOOLS IN ACTION

Now let's look at the Web sites that offer the best of these prospecting tools. In most cases you'll find several different tools at any one site. To avoid repetition, we point out only the ones that offer something unique.

### Individual Investor Online

Stock picks are a major offering of this online arm of *Individual Investor* magazine. Individual Investor Online (www.iionline.com) offers a Stock of the Day chosen by its analysts based on different investing strategies (see Figure 2.1).

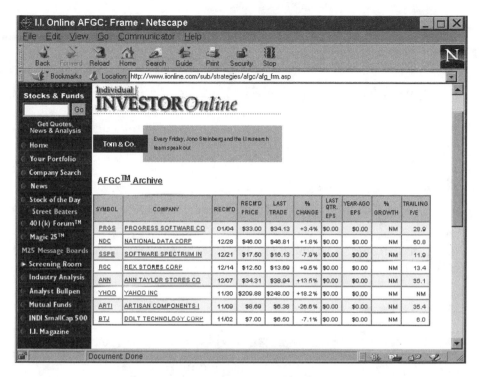

**FIGURE 2.1** The AFGC™ (America's Fastest Growing Companies) Archive from Individual Investor Online. (Source: A screen from Individual Investor Online (www.iionline.com). Copyright © 1999, Individual Investor Group, Inc. Republished with permission.)

✔ *AFGC Stocks.* Stock picks culled from America's fastest-growing companies will appeal to the growth investor. The primary requirement is that earnings per share have doubled (at least) in the most recent quarter.

✔ *Street Beaters.* Here's one for both growth and value investors: stocks with earnings surprises. They've beaten the analysts' forecasts for the most recent quarter.

✔ *Hot Stocks.* A momentum investor's choice: stocks that have recently hit new price highs or have exceptional price momentum.

✔ *Insider's Edge.* For those who think insiders are in the know, these stock picks are companies in which corporate officers or directors have recently purchased or sold shares.

✔ *Uncommon Value.* This category uncovers conservative growth stocks with limited downside risk.

✔ *Magic 25.* Individual Investor Online selects 25 of the stock picks during the year for its Magic 25 portfolio, which it claims has outperformed the averages for the past six years.

You can gauge the analysts' performance by following their stock picks or by checking out the archives. Then you'll know how much credence to give their future selections. You may also find stock picks in Individual Investor Online's industry updates.

## Market Guide Investor

Market Guide Investor (www.marketguide.com) is known for its company profiles, which we'll review in the next chapter. For stock prospecting, it has an interesting take on the hot stocks concept. With just three mouse clicks in the What's Hot/What's Not section (Figure 2.2) you can

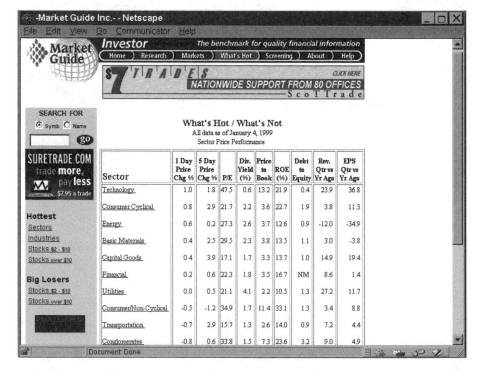

### What's Hot / What's Not
All data as of January 4, 1999
Sector Price Performance

| Sector | 1 Day Price Chg % | 5 Day Price Chg % | P/E | Div. Yield (%) | Price to Book | ROE (%) | Debt to Equity | Rev. Qtr vs Yr Ago | EPS Qtr vs Yr Ago |
|---|---|---|---|---|---|---|---|---|---|
| Technology | 1.0 | 1.8 | 47.5 | 0.6 | 13.2 | 21.9 | 0.4 | 23.9 | 36.8 |
| Consumer Cyclical | 0.8 | 2.9 | 21.7 | 2.2 | 3.6 | 22.7 | 1.9 | 3.8 | 11.3 |
| Energy | 0.6 | 0.2 | 27.3 | 2.6 | 3.7 | 12.6 | 0.9 | -12.0 | -34.9 |
| Basic Materials | 0.4 | 2.5 | 29.5 | 2.3 | 3.8 | 13.5 | 1.1 | 3.0 | -3.8 |
| Capital Goods | 0.4 | 3.9 | 17.1 | 1.7 | 3.3 | 13.7 | 1.0 | 14.9 | 19.4 |
| Financial | 0.2 | 0.6 | 22.3 | 1.8 | 3.5 | 16.7 | NM | 8.6 | 1.4 |
| Utilities | 0.0 | 0.5 | 21.1 | 4.1 | 2.2 | 10.5 | 1.3 | 27.2 | 11.7 |
| Consumer/Non-Cyclical | -0.5 | -1.2 | 34.9 | 1.7 | 11.4 | 33.1 | 1.3 | 3.4 | 8.8 |
| Transportation | -0.7 | 2.9 | 15.7 | 1.3 | 2.6 | 14.0 | 0.9 | 7.2 | 4.4 |
| Conglomerates | -0.8 | 0.6 | 33.8 | 1.5 | 7.3 | 23.6 | 3.2 | 9.0 | 4.9 |

**FIGURE 2.2** The Hottest Sectors on January 4, 1999, from Market Guide Investor. (Reprinted with permission of Market Guide, Inc.)

find the hottest stocks in the hottest *industry groups* of the hottest *sectors*! Here's how it works.

The Hottest Sectors table lists a dozen sectors in descending order of daily price change. Click on a sector to display a table of the industries that make up that sector, arranged in descending order of daily price change. Click on an industry to display a table of the companies in that industry, in—you guessed it—descending order of daily price change. At the stock tables, clicking on the stock name brings up a brief overview of the company (the Market Guide Snapshot).

Another prospecting tool is the custom stock screen, but you need to be an experienced investor to use it effectively. For now, we'll look at other screening tools that are less intimidating to the beginning investor.

### MSN Investor

MSN Investor (www.investor.msn.com) makes almost everyone's list, including ours, of the half dozen best investing sites on the Web. (It is part of the Microsoft MoneyCentral personal finance site.) The one drawback is that you have to download (free) software with older browsers to use three key tools—the portfolio, the charts, and the Investment Finder—but it takes less than five minutes. Once done, you're set until Microsoft upgrades the software (every six months or so), at which time you'll get a notice to download the new version.

 **Downloading Files**   Downloading a file or program is relatively simple, but it can be time-consuming, depending on the speed of your modem. Just click the link to the file, enter a file name when and if prompted, and wait. (Be sure to write down the file name so you can find it later.) Then follow the Web site's instructions for opening the file or installing the software. Downloading times vary, depending primarily on the speed of your modem or Internet connection. Usually, the Web site provides an estimate of download time, and most browsers display a real-time status of the download. In general, allow about one minute for each 100,000 bytes (100KB) of data with a 28.8 modem; double that time for a 14.4 modem.

MSN Investor offers an excellent source of investment ideas, one of which is the Investment Finder. The Finder offers a dozen preset screens, plus a custom screen builder. The preset screens include:

✔ The *contrarian strategy* seeks out-of-favor stocks (Figure 2.3).

✔ Dogs of the Dow uses a *Dow dividend approach* but concentrates on the cheapest five—the "dogs."

✔ This Year's Winners turns up stocks with the greatest price appreciation over the past year.

✔ Righteous Rockets looks for undervalued but fast-growing stocks with strong balance sheets that have begun to rise in price.

There are also screens for value investors, growth investors, momentum investors, and fundamental investors looking for turnarounds.

And if none of these appeals to you, you can create your own custom

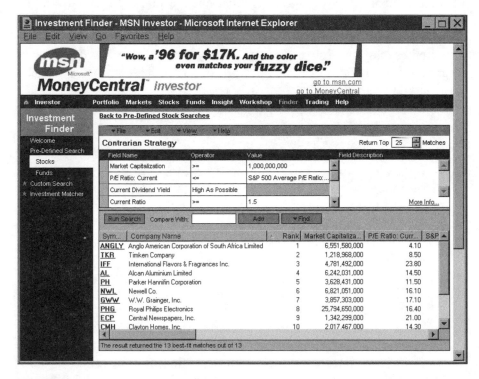

**FIGURE 2.3**  A contrarian strategy screen from MSN Investor. (Reprinted with permission of Microsoft Corporation.)

screen using any of 264 criteria. It helps if you know what you're looking for and understand the use of *operators* such as *greater than*, *less than*, or *equal to*. MSN Investor, by the way, has an excellent Help section.

> **Operators**  Symbols, such as < (less than) or > (greater than), which are used in some screening programs to qualify the factors used in the screen.

MSN Investor uses the Finder screens to create another good source of investment ideas, its Supermodels. (Look under Investment Finder.) The difference between a screen and a supermodel is this: A screen uses price, volume, and value criteria to create a list of stocks from a database; a supermodel is a list of stocks (or a portfolio) created from a screen, with buy/hold/sell recommendations for each stock.

Another source of investment ideas at this site is the Strategy Lab (Figure 2.4), which lets you peer into the minds of investment professionals as they buy and sell stocks based on four different strategies. The strategies (which may change by the time you read this) are value investing, insider trading, technology stocks, and something called *Strategic Indexing*. (There are also a fund strategy and an options strategy.) Detailed analyses are given along with buy/hold/sell recommendations. This is a good place to learn about strategies and see them in action.

Another good source for ideas is the Up/Downgrades section under Market Update. This is free, but Investment Finder and the Strategy Lab are subscription-based ($9.95/month with a 30-day free trial). You are required to enter your credit card number for the free trial, although your card is not charged. You must resubscribe at the end of 30 days to activate the account.

## The Motley Fool

The Motley Fool (www.fool.com) serves up names like the Fool's School, Fools of a Feather, Fribble, and the Dueling Fools, but lurking beneath the cutesy titles are some pretty cool prospecting tools.

For stock picks, they offer the Daily Double, a stock that has recently doubled in value (Figure 2.5), and the Daily Trouble, a stock that has recently lost half its value. Both have detailed analyses, which can be used as a jumping-off point for your own evaluation. You'll also find links to some lively message boards about the stocks.

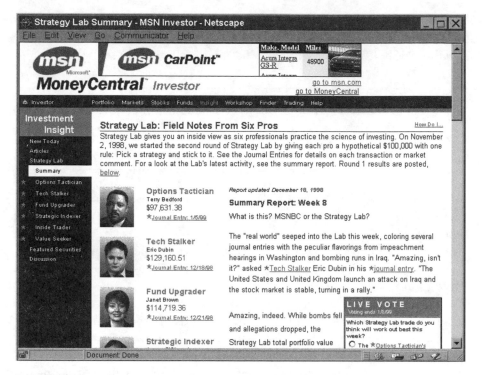

**FIGURE 2.4** The Strategy Lab at MSN Investor lets you track the effectiveness of different investing strategies as implemented by the pros. (Reprinted with permission of Microsoft Corporation.)

Stock picks also appear in the Fool's Workshop and the Dueling Fools. The latter sets two opposing analysts on one stock, rather like CNN's *Crossfire*. Another pool of investment ideas can be found in The Motley Fool's quintet of portfolios.

- ✔ *The Fool Portfolio.* A long-term, buy-and-hold portfolio.
- ✔ *Cash-King Portfolio.* A 10-stock, 10-year portfolio, with an 11-step explanation of the Cash-King approach.
- ✔ *Boring Portfolio.* The strategy is based on, in the words of its manager, "Peter Lynch's *One Up on Wall Street* meets the Gardner brothers' *The Motley Fool Investment Guide* with some of Robert Pirsig's *Zen and the Art of Motorcycle Maintenance* tossed in."
- ✔ *DRIP Portfolio.* Based on *dividend reinvestment plans (DRIPs)*, this portfolio makes small monthly investments in leading companies for the long term (20 years).

**FIGURE 2.5**   The Motley Fool's Daily Double stock pick for January 4, 1999. (Reprinted with permission of The Motley Fool, Inc.)

✔ *Foolish Four.* The Motley Fool's slant on the classic Dow dividend approach, fully explained at the site.

There are also four stock screens called "Diamonds in the Rough and Dogs in the Pound." These point-and-click screens scan a database of earnings announcements to filter out (1) companies that have exceeded the analysts' earnings estimates and (2) companies with sales and earnings growth greater than 15 percent and increasing margins. (For shorting stocks, there are mirror screens for companies missing their estimates or with decreasing margins.)

## PersonalWealth.com

This flagship site of Standard & Poor's (www.personalwealth.com) overflows with investment ideas. (Look under Stocks.) Here are just a few:

**STARS**  STARS stands for Stock Appreciation Ranking System. One to five stars are awarded based on S&P's assessment of the stock's potential for price growth. Stocks with five stars are expected to be the best short-term performers in six months to a year.

✔ *S&P's Managed Portfolios.*  You'll find some of the brightest stars in S&P's managed portfolios. Three of the portfolios are based on the S&P STARS ranking system; the other two are undervalued stocks and small caps/IPOs. The beauty of portfolios, of course, is that you can track their performance over time.

✔ *STARS Picks and Pans* and *Word on the Street.*  These highlight recent upgrades, downgrades, and changes in earnings estimates.

✔ *Stock of the Week.*  A stock is selected from the universe of stocks outside the S&P STARS system. A brief analysis is offered but no buy-sell recommendation from the analyst. S&P urges viewers to analyze the stock thoroughly before purchasing it (and we concur).

✔ *Stock Screens.*  S&P preconfigures and runs one screen each week. The viewer is presented with a short list of stocks from the screen, along with a very brief look at the criteria used. You can view the archive of the past month's screens, but you can't run any of the screens yourself.

✔ *Market Movers.*  The biggest gainers (or losers) of the day are spotlighted.

✔ *Takeover Talk.*  This is one of the few places on the Web to get an informed list of companies that have announced mergers or acquisitions or are rumored to be *in play*. Brief explanations of the deal or potential deal are included.

**Investing Supersites**  Investing supersites are those that cover all or most of the investing spectrum. We mention them repeatedly in these pages because they usually have the best or the most unique investing tools. Most of the sites mentioned in this chapter are considered investing supersites.

S&P welcomes registered viewers, but most features of value are reserved for subscribers, at $9.95 a month.

## Wall Street City

Another big hitter is Wall Street City (www.wallstreetcity.com), the online arm of Telescan, Inc. Wall Street City (WSC) offers the widest range of stock screens and search products on the Net. Powered by the same engine that drives Telescan's offline superstar ProSearch, Wall Street City's screens and searches include:

✔ *Triple Screen Top 20 List.* WSC pulls out three big guns for these screens: ProSearch, back-tested searches, and its What's Working Now feature. It uses a series of screens to come up with "the best of the best"; sometimes only a handful of stocks make it through the gauntlet. The screens are described in the What's Working Now center under Analysis & Commentary.

 **What's Working Now** This is a massive, automatic back-testing system that generates artificially developed searches showing the best return in recent months.

✔ *Technical Screens.* Prebuilt technical screens include *breakouts*—basing pattern breakouts and positive short-term technical breakouts.

 **breakout** a change in a technical indicator that generates a change in the trading signal, from a hold to a buy or sell, from a buy to a sell, or from a sell to a buy.

✔ *Custom Searches.* WSC's *Java*-based ProSearch offers more than 700 criteria for creating custom stock searches. Once you decide on the general strategy, building the screen is easy. Just select the indicators (up to 30) and give each a value by clicking on a button or entering a minimum and maximum range. You can also simply display the value for an indicator, without affecting the search. Along with the list of stocks found by the search is a chart that displays the back-tested results.

**Java** A computer language designed by Sun Microsystems that uses moving text, animation, and interactivity. Some older browsers are not "Java-enabled."

✔ *Back-Tested Searches.* These prebuilt searches—*back-tested* on previous market data—have turned up winning lists of stocks, many of which have been published by Telescan. The assumption is that the same searches should perform equally well in today's market assuming market conditions are similar or continue in the same vein. There are a dozen categories (Figure 2.6), each of which offers two to ten screens that you can run yourself on current market data. The search report contains the top 25 stocks on the day of the search, along with the back-tested results (Figure 2.7) that show the percent gain or loss over 12 months for the top 50 stocks.

**Back-Testing** Telescan back-tests searches by running the search on the first day of each month for the past 12 months and plotting the performance of the top 25 stocks from each search to the current day. (The back-testing chart slopes from left to right because the more recent stocks have had less time to perform.) The objective is to find searches that perform well consistently.

There are too many investment ideas at this site to describe each one. You'll have to check them out yourself. Most of the screens and searches are subscription-based ($34.95/month), but first check out the 30-day free trial.

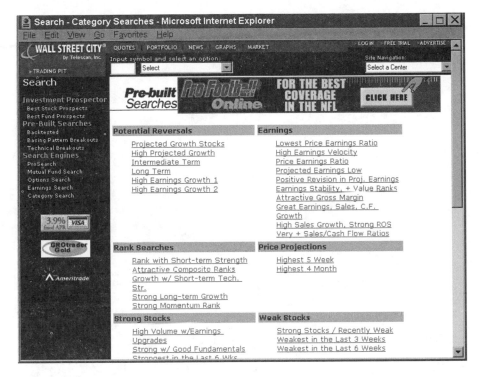

**FIGURE 2.6** These are a few of the categories for back-tested searches at Wall Street City. (Reprinted with permission of Telescan, Inc.)

**Prices Trending Lower** Subscription prices and free features may well change over the next few months. Investing Web sites are trending toward lower prices and more free tools.

## And Consider These . . .

There are dozens of other Web sites that offer investment ideas. Consider these:

**SmartMoney.com** This Dow Jones–owned site (www.smartmoney.com) has a potpourri of picks, portfolios, and screens. A full discussion of each screen is given ("the recipe"), and the stock pick from the Daily Screen is

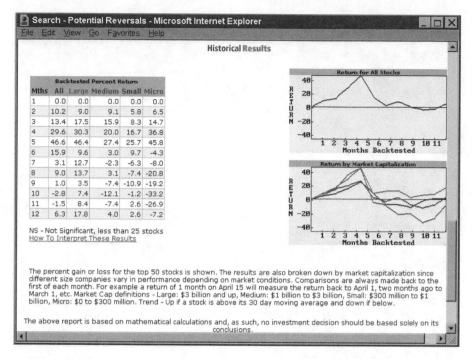

**FIGURE 2.7** Each back-tested search at Wall Street City displays historical results by market capitalization. (Reprinted with permission of Telescan, Inc.)

analyzed in depth. Be sure to check out the archived screens. By the way, stock data (more than is displayed in the screen) can be downloaded into Excel or another spreadsheet.

**Equis International** Technicians will appreciate the free technical screens from the creator of MetaStock (www.equis.com). (Click Hot Stocks on the left navigation bar.) Fourteen screens tap a database of some 2200 optionable securities (based on the previous day's closing data). If you know (or care) what "bullish engulfing pattern" or "breaking out of consolidation" means, then you've found yourself a good prospecting tool.

**Hoover's Online** This Austin-based publisher of company profiles (www.hoovers.com) offers a Company of the Day and a Spotlight Stock. There's also a custom stock screener, which allows the user to specify minimum and maximum ranges for 20 criteria. Take care not to make the ranges too restrictive. Otherwise, you'll eliminate all possible candidates.

**Zacks Investment Research** If you believe in the prescient power of earnings estimates, you might want to subscribe to Zacks, the premier provider of same. Zacks' Analyst Watch on the Internet (www.zacks.com) costs about $150 a year and gives you access to, among other things, online screening with 80 or more earnings-based criteria and the Z-100 list of stocks handpicked by Len Zacks.

## SUMMARY

Prospecting for stocks on the Net can be fun. But, you may end up with a very long list of prospective candidates. Obviously, you'll have to make some choices, unless you've got a money tree in your backyard. The only way to choose the best stocks from a list of good ones is to do your homework: Research and evaluate each stock. We'll show you how to do it online in the next chapter.

## WEB SITES FOR INVESTMENT IDEAS

| | |
|---|---|
| Equis International | www.equis.com |
| Hoover's Online | www.hoovers.com |
| Individual Investor Online | www.iionline.com |
| Market Guide Investor | www.marketguide.com |
| The Motley Fool | www.fool.com |
| MSN Investor | www.investor.msn.com |
| PersonalWealth.com | www.personalwealth.com |
| Quicken.com | www.quicken.com/investments |
| SmartMoney.com | www.smartmoney.com |
| StockSite | www.stocksite.com |
| Trend Trader | www.trendtrader.com |
| Wall Street City | www.wallstreetcity.com |
| Zacks Investment Research | www.zacks.com |

**Tired of Typing URLs?** For your convenience, alphabetized links to the Web sites mentioned in each chapter can be found at www.cyberinvest.com. Click Book Links on the home page.

# Doing Your Homework
## Checking Facts,
## Pondering Patterns

---

**M**ost people wouldn't think of buying a house or a used car on someone else's word. They would do a little homework first: Drive through the neighborhood and check out recent house sales. Get a third-party appraisal and inspection report. Check out *Consumer's Guide* ratings of the best used cars. Run the best candidate past the trained eye of a mechanic.

Yet it is not uncommon for a beginning investor to sink thousands of dollars into a stock based on someone else's hot tip.

It is a foolish and unnecessary risk—especially when you can now do your own homework by tapping into the vast investing resources on the Internet.

Doing your homework boils down to two basic steps. The first involves a quick study of the company's current condition and a review of the forecasts about its future—take its temperature, so to speak. The second step is to look at the stock's trading patterns—read the charts. Neither is as difficult as it might sound, given the tools available on the Internet.

The first step is called *fundamental analysis*. This means looking at a few key *financial ratios*, the earnings history, and the company's potential for future growth according to those who know the company best.

The second step is called *technical analysis*. In its simplest form, which is all we're going to talk about in this book, this involves looking at price-and-volume charts to see whether now is a good time to buy the stock. Even investors who swear by a company's fundamentals can improve their potential for profits—in our experience, by up to three percentage points—if they use a couple of technical signals to time the purchase of a fundamentally sound stock.

**Fundamental Analysis**  Evaluating a stock by assessing a company's intrinsic worth and growth potential based on such factors as historical earnings, projected earnings, revenues, cash flow, and various financial ratios.

Fortunately, the Internet has taken the drudgery out of such homework and placed everything you need at the tip of your mouse.

We have divided this discussion into two sections: one devoted to a company's fundamentals and one devoted to charts and technical timing signals. In the fundamental section, we explore briefly how to measure a company's basic health and potential for growth. Then we examine the online tools for taking these measurements. Finally, we show you where to find the tools on the Net.

**Technical Analysis**  Evaluating the price potential of a security by studying price-and-volume patterns, using any of dozens of technical indicators.

In the technical section, we talk about a couple of technical tools that can give you a sense of when to purchase or not purchase a stock. Then we show you where on the Net to find such tools. For the sake of brevity, we have kept the theoretical discussion brief and to the point. If you want to learn more about fundamental or technical analysis, our sister publication, *Getting Started in Technical Analysis* by Jack Schwager, is a good place to start.

Before we get to the real homework, let's look at a couple of tools that could almost eliminate the need for in-depth research. At the very least, they can take some of the work out of homework.

# SNAPSHOTS OF A STOCK

Computers make it possible to store massive amounts of data and retrieve it with a click of a mouse. But they do much more than that. In nanoseconds, Pentium processors can scan millions of pieces of data and perform hundreds of thousands of calculations that would take us mere mortals weeks or months to do. Here are some tools that use these kinds of scans to give you an instantaneous snapshot of a stock.

## Ranking Snapshots

One of the coolest tools for evaluating stocks is the rankings snapshot at Wall Street City (www.wallstreetcity.com—Figure 3.1).

As in MRI (magnetic resonance imaging), the snapshot scans the inner workings of a stock and presents a colorful graph of its findings. The horizontal bars on the graph are color coded. The red bars on the left represent the lower 50 percent of all stocks; the green bars on the right represent the upper 50 percent of all stocks. The little gold triangle on each bar indicates where the stock falls within the range for each of 11 rankings; the percentile figure is shown in the middle column.

Each ranking is a composite of several different indicators. (Click the Rank Type to see what it's made of.) Long-term growth, for example, is made up of eight earnings, sales, and cash flow indicators; fundamental rank comprises a company's current ratio, debt-to-equity ratio, cash-to-price ratio, cash flow growth, and interest coverage. Volume rank is basically a money flow indicator based on different volume ratios.

**Other Stock Scans** You can also scan a stock for analysts' ratings and insider trading in the portfolio section at Wall Street City. See Chapter 4.

## Advisor FYI Alerts

MSN Investor (www.investor.msn.com) offers another helpful tool to reduce your homework: the Advisor FYI. This feature generates alerts about events that may affect a stock, including analyst projections, company financials, news, and stock performance patterns. Unlike most portfolio alerts, Advisor FYI stores a company's alerts for several months, so you

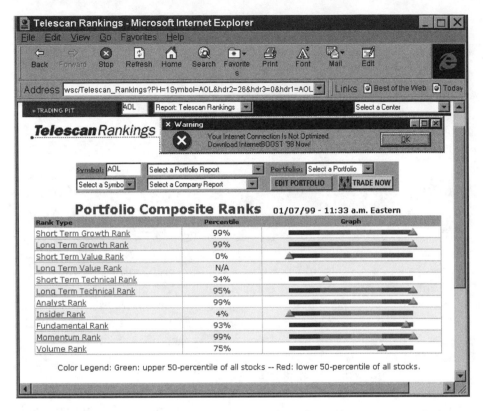

**FIGURE 3.1** This Telescan Rankings snapshot shows how America Online (AOL) ranks against all other stocks in 11 categories. (Reprinted with permission of Telescan, Inc.)

can see the important recent events. This makes it possible to use it for stock research. For a company like Yahoo! the alerts can run into the dozens on any given day (Figure 3.2).

Microsoft cautions against using the alerts as buy or sell signals and says they should be used as a starting point for further homework. We emphatically concur! The rest of this chapter will help you find the fundamental and technical tools for doing that homework.

 **FYI Portfolio Alerts**  Advisor FYI can be used with an MSN Investor portfolio. Stocks in the portfolio will be flagged when an alert is received.

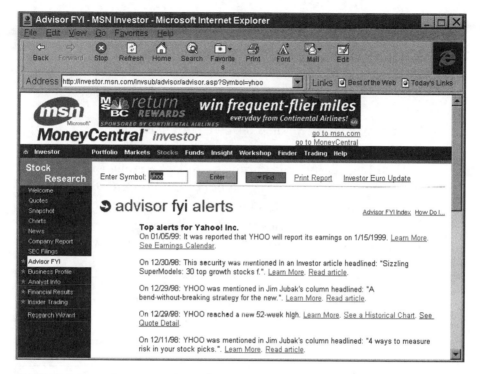

**FIGURE 3.2**   Advisor FYI alerts for Yahoo! on January 5, 1999, from MSN Investor. (Reprinted with permission of Microsoft Corporation.)

## LOOKING AT A COMPANY'S FUNDAMENTALS

A handful of key ratios can tell you whether a company is basically healthy and has potential for future growth. Here are nine important fundamental indicators, along with some tips on how to judge them if you're buying *long*. The weight you give each one—and whether you include it in your evaluation—depends on your investing style.

1. Study the trend in *historical earnings*. The growth rate of earnings over the past five to ten years should be as high as possible, preferably over 15 percent.

2. Check current and recent earnings, looking for a solid increase in *quarter-over-quarter earnings*. It's even better if the company beats the analysts' quarterly estimates.

**Quarter-over-Quarter Earnings**  A comparison of a company's current quarterly earnings per share with its earnings per share for the same quarter last year.

3. How do *projected earnings* relate to current earnings? Pay attention to the projected five-year *earnings per share (EPS)* growth rate.

4. Regarding the price-to-earnings ratio, the growth rate over the past five to ten years *or the projected five-year growth rate* should be equal to or greater than the P/E ratio.

5. *Price-to-sales ratio* varies tremendously from industry to industry. It should be in line with other stocks in the industry.

**Price-to-Sales Ratio**  A company's stock price divided by its annual sales.

**Industry Comparisons**  Comparison of a company's financial ratios with its industry is usually found on the company snapshot or profile.

6. Price-to-book ratio, as with sales-to-price ratio, should be in line with the industry.

7. *Dividend yield* is important only if you're counting on income from your stocks.

8. Note any *insider trading*. Studies have shown that insider buying is a very good indicator of future stock growth.

9. Watch for recent or breaking news that might impact the stock.

**Fundamental Snapshot**  Most of these fundamental ratios and figures are reflected in the Telescan Rankings snapshot described earlier.

These figures and ratios are available in a few key documents: company profiles, earnings estimate reports, insider trading reports, and corporate news. (Often, these are combined into one report.) At investing supersites a list of available reports pops up when you get a stock quote or graph, and all you have to do is point and click.

There are other tools, such as in-depth research reports and SEC filings, for those who care to dig that deeply. We prefer to let someone like Standard & Poor's or Market Guide do the work for us. These companies, and others like them, produce the streamlined company profiles that summarize and explain everything you really need to know about a company to make an informed stock purchase.

Let's take a look at the major reports.

## Company Profiles: The Long and the Short of It

Most of your homework can be done with a good company profile. These are reports compiled by a number of independent third parties, such as Market Guide, Standard & Poor's, Disclosure, Thomson, Hoover's, and Baseline. These profilers assimilate raw data from *10Ks*, *10Qs*, and independent *research reports* and come up with easy-to-grasp summaries, tables, ratios, and projections for each of the 3,000 to 12,000 public companies in their databases. Because they use the same sources, the major difference among the profilers is the presentation of the data.

**10K** The annual report filed by public companies with the SEC, which provides a comprehensive overview of the company. The report must be filed within 90 days after the end of the company's fiscal year.

**10Q** A quarterly report filed by public companies with the SEC which contains unaudited financial statements. The 10Q must be filed within 45 days of the close of first, second, and third quarters of the company's fiscal year.

Most offer long and short versions of company profiles. The short one, usually free, summarizes a company's vital statistics, like the Market

**FIGURE 3.3**  Market Guide Snapshot for Netscape Communications.
(Reprinted with permission of Market Guide, Inc.)

Guide snapshot in Figure 3.3. These are helpful in the way that a snapshot is helpful when you're contemplating a blind date: It puts a face on the person but it tells you nothing about personality, character, or background or even whether the potential date is tall or short.

The longer company profiles include detailed information about the type of business and industry, current and historical financials and stock prices, institutional ownership, capital structure, insider trading, *short interest*, and dozens of financial ratios. Usually, the information is presented in easy-to-read tables, charts, and graphs. These longer reports are usually subscription- or fee-based.

Let's look at the major names you'll find on investing Web sites: Market Guide, Standard & Poor's, Hoover's, Thomson, Disclosure, and Baseline.

**Market Guide**  Market Guide supplies reports to many investing Web sites, which frequently charge for everything except the snapshot. But—at the

**Short Interest** The number of a company's shares that have been sold short and not yet repurchased, frequently reported as the number of days it would take to cover the short position, assuming the volume of stock stays at its average volume traded over the past 30 days.

time this chapter is being written—Market Guide itself (www.marketguide. com) offers several free snapshots that provide a fairly rounded view of a company. They include:

- ✔ Snapshot (Figure 3.3): a brief overview of the company with key ratios and statistics.
- ✔ Price performance history and comparison, plus short interest analysis.
- ✔ Highlights of growth rates, revenues, and EPS.
- ✔ Comparisons of dozens of ratios with the industry, sector, and the S&P 500.
- ✔ Selected items from the income statement, balance sheet, and cash flow statement.

**Standard & Poor's** One of best-known names in stock research is Standard & Poor's (S&P). In addition to the standard data, S&P offers a *STARS ranking system* for about 4500 of the 10,000 listed and NASDAQ stocks. Stocks are ranked from one to five based on S&P's assessment of the stock's potential for price growth. Stocks with five stars are expected to be the best short-term performers in six months to a year; stocks with one star, the worst. The STARS rankings are part of the S&P stock report, which is now called Enhanced Analytics.

S&P's personal investor site is PersonalWealth.com (www.personal wealth.com). The monthly site subscription of $9.95 includes 20 Enhanced Analytics per month, or you may purchase them online for $1 each.

**Hoover's Profiles** Hoover's, Inc. profiles more than 3000 of "the world's largest, fastest growing and most influential enterprises." (Their words.) A free company snapshot is offered at the site (www.hoovers.com), but a full report is available when you subscribe to the site (12.95/month).

**Thomson Reports** Company reports from Thomson Financial Services incorporate information from such Thomson subsidiaries as First Call (news and earnings estimates), CDA/Investnet (insider trading activity), CDA/Spectrum (institutional holdings), and Investext (professional research reports). Thomson Investors Network supplies reports to other investing and broker sites, but also has its own subscription-based site at www.thomsoninvest.com for $34.95/year. The site subscription includes 25 company reports and 25 mutual fund reports a year. Premium packages are $19.95/month for First Call's earnings estimates and $19.95/month for insider trading reports, or $300/year for both.

**Disclosure Reports** Disclosure produces company reports for some 12,000 U.S. public companies and 13,000 global companies. You'll see them on various investing sites, and you can download the reports on a pay-per-view basis at the Disclosure site (www.disclosure-investor.com). (The Profile Tearsheet costs $3; the Investment Tearsheet, $5.) You can also access free (delayed) *EDGAR* filings.

**EDGAR** An acronym for the SEC's paperless filing system for public companies. It stands for Electronic Data Gathering, Analysis and Retrieval. EDGAR filings include 10Ks and 10Qs, but the SEC reports that 95 percent of all insider transactions are still filed in paper form.

**Baseline Profiles** Baseline profiles differ from other company profiles in the extensive use of charts and graphs to illuminate a company's fundamental and stock performance data (Figure 3.4). Baseline's own Web site is aimed at institutional investors (www.baseline.com), but it supplies reports to other Web sites and broker sites. You can also purchase Baseline reports on a pay-per-view or subscription basis at Wall Street Research Net (www.wsrn.com) and WallSt.com (www.wallst.com).

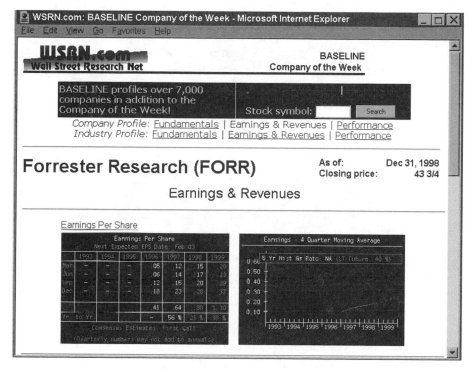

**FIGURE 3.4** A Baseline report includes charts and graphs for earnings per share, P/E range, earnings surprises, and revenues. (Reprinted with permission of Wall Street Research Net.)

## The Importance of Earnings Estimates

One of the most important harbingers of future stock price is a consensus change in earnings estimates by industry *analysts*. These analysts, who work for full-service brokerages or institutional investors, conduct extensive research and in-depth analysis of an industry and the companies in that industry. Then they produce reports about the industry and the current condition and growth potential of the companies. There may be only one analyst following a company, or there may be dozens in the case of a company like Microsoft or IBM.

For the companies they follow, analysts make projections about earnings for the current and next quarter and current and next fiscal year. In some cases, they project a five-year growth rate. Then they make recommendations on whether to buy, sell, or hold the stock.

Such information was formerly available only to professional investors. Now, it's yours for the taking.

Zacks Investment Research, I/B/E/S, and First Call Corporation are the main providers of earnings estimates to investing sites and broker sites. These companies compile the figures that reflect the consensus of all the analysts that follow a company and present them in various tables, charts, and summaries.

All three companies supply earnings estimates reports to other Web sites and broker sites, but they also have their own Web sites.

✔ *Zacks* (www.zacks.com—Figure 3.5) offers its reports to individual investors through its Analysts Watch on the Internet. For $150 a year you'll get the following for some 6000 companies:

Company summary information.

Price/volume data.

Analysts buy/hold/sell recommendations.

Current EPS estimates and distribution of estimates.

History of earnings surprises.

Financial history.

EPS history.

Company versus industry growth rates.

Financial ratios and comparisons with industry.

The subscription also includes a portfolio tracker, screening software with 200 criteria, and online screening with 81 earnings-based criteria.

✔ *First Call* (www.firstcall.com), a division of Thomson Financial Services, offers its reports by fax or on the Internet on a pay-per-piece basis ($1.50 to $6 each).

✔ *I/B/E/S* (www.ibes.com) offers estimates on 18,000 stocks in 52 countries. Subscriptions for individual investors range from $9.95 a month for a basic U.S. service to $49.95 for enhanced global services.

Keep in mind that most company profiles include the consensus estimates and buy/hold/sell recommendations, so it isn't necessary to purchase these separately. Also, many investing supersites include the Zacks or First Call reports as part of their site subscriptions. As you become acquainted with online investing, you will see that one or two sources are all you'll need. In order to make those choices, however, you should be aware of the full range of online investing possibilities. That is the purpose of this book.

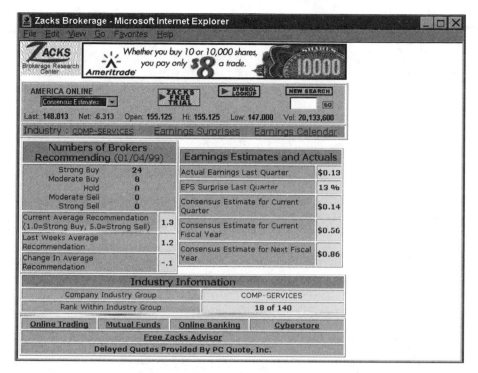

**FIGURE 3.5** Consensus estimates for America Online from Zacks Investment Research. (Reprinted with permission of Zacks Investment Research.)

## Insiders: Should You Follow Their Lead?

In his book *One Up on Wall Street*, Peter Lynch says, "There's no better tip-off to the probable success of a stock than that people in the company are putting their own money into it." Various studies—and common sense—support this statement. Why else would *corporate insiders* buy their company's stock? They know the inner workings of the company, so it stands to reason that if they're shelling out their own dollars for the stock, they believe it's going to go up. (Insider selling, on the other hand, is frequently just an indication that executives are using stock options to pay their bills.)

The availability of insider trading reports is another sign of the crumbling barriers between the professional and individual investor. What used to require teams of researchers sifting through SEC reports filed by corporate insiders is now available on many investing Web sites, courtesy of Vickers Stock Research Corporation (www.argusgroup.com)

or CDA Investnet (a division of the Thomson Financial Services) (www.cda.com/investnet).

Bob Gabele, who is president of CDA Investnet, is a recognized industry expert on insider trading analysis. He offers the following at the Thomson Web site (www.thomsoninvest.com), all based on insider trading:

✔ Tip of the Day (free) (Figure 3.6).

✔ Stock of the Day (free) with a brief analysis.

✔ Insider's Periscope (free), which highlights stocks that insiders are accumulating.

✔ Insider's Chronicle—an online weekly newsletter that offers analysis and commentary on specific insider trading. Subscription is $19.95/month ($199.95/year), which includes the Thomson site subscription.

**FIGURE 3.6** Bob Gabele of Thomson Investors Network offers a Tip of the Day based on insider trading. (Reprinted with permission of Thomson Investors Network; © Thomson Investors Network.)

Another site with a unique twist on insider trading is Wall Street City (www.wallstreetcity.com). You can use insider trading as a search indicator *and* scan your portfolio for insider activity (more about this in Chapter 4). You can also plot insider trading on a long-term stock graph, which reflects how accurate insiders have been in the past. All are part of the Level 2 $19.95/month subscription.

### Searching the News

Your homework isn't complete until you've checked the news on a company. After all, the latest company profile or earnings report might be several weeks old. The news is the only way you can find out if something has happened recently—or is about to happen—that might affect the stock price.

On the Internet, searching for news is like looking for sand on the beach. Most supersites and all news sites have changing headlines throughout the day and a searchable news database. Most sites get their news feeds from a handful of news sources, such as Reuters, Associated Press, and others, so you'll find the same or similar stories at any of these sites. To retrieve the recent news stories on a company, all you have to do is enter a stock symbol. Often, the stories have links to related stories as well. By the time you've surfed all the links you'll know all the recent news about the stock.

If you want to find past articles on a stock, you might want to try ZDNet (www.zdnet.com), which archives articles back to 1996 (Figure 3.7). You can narrow your search to a specific topic and time frame by clicking More Options on the search page, a useful feature not offered by many sites. Even better, it's free. A more costly alternative is The Wall Street Journal Interactive Edition ($29.95/year for print subscribers; $59.95 for nonsubscribers, which also gets you into Barron's Online). The Journal archives articles for only 30 days; if you want to go further back, you can search the "top business publications" on a cost-per-article basis ($2.95 each).

 **Related Stories**    Look for links to related stories, definitions, Web sites, and other online material in all Web documents.

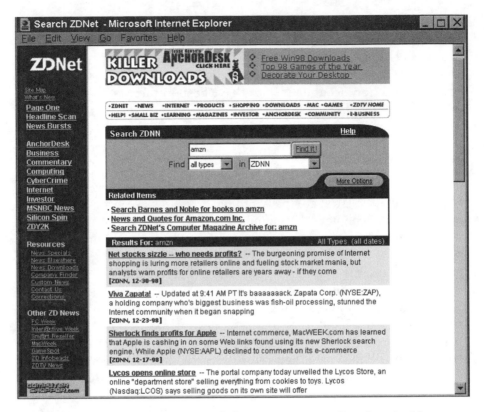

**FIGURE 3.7** A ZDNet news search for Amazon.com. (Reprinted with permission of ZDNet.)

Your homework up to this point has been based on a company's fundamentals. Now we're going to look at a few simple ways to check out a stock's technical trading patterns. Paying attention to when you buy a stock—with an eye toward optimum technical patterns—can add from one to three percentage points to your overall returns. And interpreting technical patterns is not as hard as it might sound.

## LOOKING AT TECHNICAL PATTERNS

The subject of technical analysis is too vast to be considered here. But it is obvious that the optimum time to purchase a stock—to minimize risk and maximize return—is near the beginning of an uptrend, or at least when the trend is strengthening rather than weakening.

We can show you a few basic technical patterns that will help you determine the optimum entry point for a stock. The tools for discerning these patterns include support and resistance lines, rising and falling trend lines, basing pattern breakouts, trading bands, and the MACD indicator. A quick look at these patterns can help you distinguish between a good and a bad entry point in a stock.

## Support and Resistance Lines

One of the few Web sites that offer charts on which you can draw support and resistance lines and trend lines is Reuters Moneynet (www.money net.com). Reuters owns Equis International, the makers of the popular technical analysis software MetaStock. Both Moneynet and the Equis International site (www.equis.com) offer Java-based charts based on MetaStock.

Support and resistance lines are among the most basic technical analysis tools. A *support* line is drawn horizontally through stock bottoms and represents a level at which the stock price has reversed in the past. In Figure 3.8, IBM shows three support levels, at $97, $110, and $120. If a stock falls to a support level and reverses direction, as IBM did in early October, the support has held and that support level is strengthened. Bouncing off a support line in this way can be a good point of entry *if* there are other positive technical signals.

 **Support** A price level that represents a floor for falling stock prices. It is a price at which buying has historically entered, thereby tending to limit declines below this level.

A *resistance* line is drawn horizontally through stock tops and represents a price barrier that is difficult for a stock to penetrate. In Figure 3.9 Mobil shows a strong resistance at about $81. Breaking through that resistance on strong volume would be very positive, but we would wait until the momentum is established before jumping in.

## Simple Trend Lines

Interpreting *trend lines* can be very complex. Just take a look at any number of books on the subject. But simple rising trend lines (drawn diago-

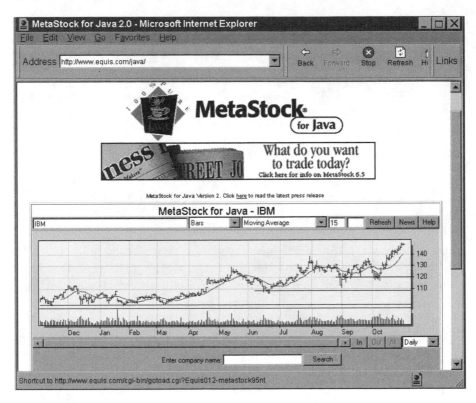

**FIGURE 3.8** In this graph IBM shows strong long-term support at about $97, with short-term support levels of about $110 and $120. (Source: Metastock for Java from Equis International, Inc. Reprinted with permission.)

**Resistance** A price level that represents a barrier for continued upward movement because in the past the stock price has stopped rising at this level and either moved sideways or reversed direction. Strong momentum is needed to push the stock through a strong resistance level.

nally through stock bottoms) and falling trend lines (drawn diagonally through stock tops) are easy to draw, easy to understand, and can help you find good entry and exit points in a stock.

The rising trend line represents a support zone; the falling trend line,

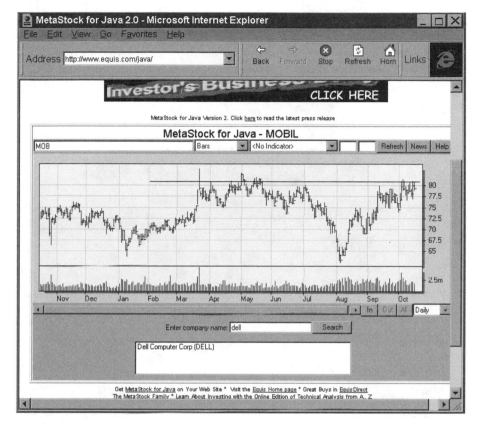

**FIGURE 3.9** In mid-October 1998 Mobil Oil Corporation was testing a strong resistance level of about $81. (Source: Metastock for Java from Equis International, Inc. Reprinted with permission.)

 **Trend Line** A line on a stock graph that connects a series of highs or lows to delineate an uptrend (representing support) or a downtrend (representing resistance).

a resistance level. A good time to buy during a rising trend is when the stock touches the rising trend line—hits support—and reverses direction to continue its upward trend, as Yahoo! did in October 1998 (Figure 3.10). A good time to consider selling is when a stock drops below a rising trend line.

**FIGURE 3.10** Yahoo! had a strong upward trend throughout September 1998. It fell through that support in early October but appears to have regained its footing as of October 17, 1998. (Source: Metastock for Java from Equis International, Inc. Reprinted with permission.)

Falling trend lines track the downward trend of a stock and form a line of resistance. When a stock breaks through this resistance, as Netscape did in Figure 3.11, it is a positive sign, especially if the *trend break* is confirmed by other signals. When a trend break occurs on large volume, its significance increases. No technical signal should be considered in isolation, however, trend lines included.

## Basing Pattern Breakouts

When a stock trades within a narrow price range for several days or weeks, as King World Productions did during the first half of October

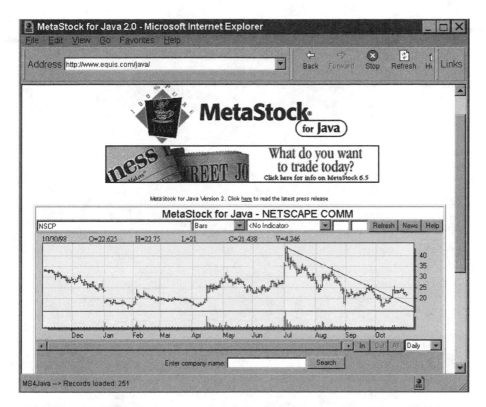

**FIGURE 3.11** Like most Internet stocks, Netscape was on a downtrend in late summer and early fall 1998. In mid-October, however, it broke through that resistance. (Source: Metastock for Java from Equis International, Inc. Reprinted with permission.)

1998 (Figure 3.12), support and resistance lines are close together. During that time, supply and demand are fairly equally matched, and the stock seems to go nowhere, *basing* within a fairly narrow price range.

The basing period itself is not very interesting, but breaking out of a basing period *upward* can be a very powerful buy signal, particularly for short-term trading.

Here are three characteristics of a good basing period breakout:

✔ The basing pattern was a tight one: The stock traded in a short range (say 10 percent) over a long period (say 26 weeks).

✔ The breakout is a half point or more.

✔ The breakout is accompanied by high volume.

**FIGURE 3.12** King World Productions was basing within a very tight range during the first two weeks of October 1998. (Source: Metastock for Java from Equis International, Inc. Reprinted with permission.)

## Trading Bands

A stock tends to trade within a predictable range around its moving average, so goes the trading bands concept. To delineate that range and form the trading bands, an envelope is drawn a certain percentage distance above and below the stock's moving average.

Trading patterns within the bands can reveal the strengths and weaknesses of the stock, although interpreting these patterns is not an exact science (nor is any technical analysis!). We use trading bands primarily to confirm an MACD buy signal (up next). There are three good confirmations:

✔ A failure swing at the bottom band: the stock approaches the bottom band and reverses without touching the band.

✔ Bouncing off the moving average after penetrating the top band.

✔ A fresh penetration of the top band.

Another pattern that indicates strength is *"climbing the band"* when the stock trades near the upper band for a period of time (Figure 3.13).

Bollinger bands, shown in Figure 3.13, are a variation on the trading bands concept developed by technical analyst John Bollinger. Bollinger bands are drawn a certain number of *standard deviations* on either side of a 20-day moving average.

Several sites offer Bollinger bands, including BigCharts (www.

**FIGURE 3.13** In this chart, Microsoft was climbing the band from early June to mid-July. In early October, it penetrated the bottom band but seems to have recovered as of October 17, 1998. (Reprinted with permission of BigCharts, Inc.)

bigcharts.com), Ask Research (www.askresearch.com), and IQNet (www.iqc.com). Of the three, BigCharts offers the most customization, with time frames from one day to maximum data, 42 indicators, and several different chart styles.

## The MACD

The moving average convergence/divergence indicator (MACD) was developed by Gerald Appel as a market timing indicator, and it is a personal favorite because it has back tested so well. The MACD uses three *exponential moving averages*: one for a short period, one for a longer period, and one for the difference between the two, which forms a signal line. In an 8-17-9 MACD, the short average is 8 days, the long average is 17 days, and the signal line is a 9-day average of their difference.

**Exponential Moving Average**   A moving average smooths the fluctuations in stock prices by averaging the prices over a specified period. An exponential moving average gives heavier weight to the most recent data.

It is difficult to find a good high-resolution MACD graph or histogram on the Web; true technicians will probably stick with technical analysis software until Web technology catches up. The best one we've found is at ClearStation (www.clearstation.com), which we like because it plots the MACD histogram as well as the MACD graph, along with a stochastic graph (Figure 3.14). We prefer the MACD histogram because signals are easier to read. ClearStation provides links to detailed explanations of how to interpret the technical charts.

**MACD Buy and Sell Signals**   A buy signal is given when the striped area moves above the zero line into positive territory—a positive breakout. A sell signal is given when the striped area dips below the signal line into negative territory—a negative breakout.

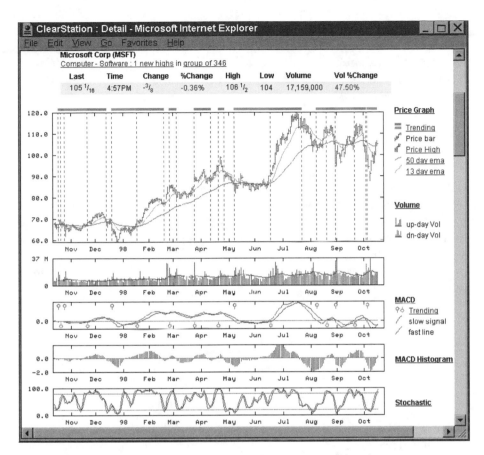

**FIGURE 3.14** Below the main graph are a volume graph, MACD graph, MACD histogram, and a stochastic graph. Click the links for help in interpreting the graphs. (Reprinted with permission of ClearStation, Inc.)

The daily MACD can give a lot of false signals when the histogram moves rapidly back and forth across the zero line. To avoid these *whip-saws*, many short-term traders require that the weekly MACD be positive before they act on a daily MACD signal. Others use the stochastic as the signal and the MACD to confirm a trend.

In the end, it is not necessary to be a technician or to understand the intricacies of technical theory. Just pay attention to the basic signals of support and resistance, and practice plotting a few indicators and watching their signals. Then settle on one you trust for your basic signal and use one or two others for confirmation.

For those who wish to learn more about technical analysis,

ClearStation, Wall Street City, Equity Analytics (www.e-analytics.com), and Technical Analysis of Stocks & Commodities (www.traders.com) offer free articles on technical indicators. Traders Library (www.traders library.com) has an extensive online bookstore of technical publications.

## SUMMARY

The key to doing effective homework is to strike a balance between doing too much and too little; too much and you confuse yourself, too little and you can make serious mistakes. Everything you need to make an informed decision can be found at any investing supersite or even at some online broker sites. So don't feel compelled to spend an inordinate amount of money or time at this step. In the end, you just need to feel comfortable enough to place the order, and only you can determine how much homework that requires.

## WEB SITES FOR EVALUATING A STOCK

| | |
|---|---|
| Ask Research | www.askresearch.com |
| Barron's Online | www.barrons.com |
| Baseline | www.baseline.com |
| BigCharts | www.bigcharts.com |
| CDA Investnet | www.cda.com/investnet |
| ClearStation | www.clearstation.com |
| Disclosure | www.disclosure-investor.com |
| Equis International | www.equis.com |
| Equity Analytics | www.e-analytics.com |
| First Call | www.firstcall.com |
| Hoover's Online | www.hoovers.com |
| I/B/E/S | www.ibes.com |
| Individual Investor Online | www.iionline.com |
| IQNet | www.iqc.com |
| Market Guide Investor | www.marketguide.com |
| MSN Investor | www.investor.msn.com |
| PersonalWealth.com | www.personalwealth.com |

| | |
|---|---|
| Reuters Moneynet | www.moneynet.com |
| Technical Analysis of Stocks & Commodities | www.traders.com |
| Thomson Investors Network | www.thomsoninvest.com |
| Traders Library | www.traderslibrary.com |
| Vickers Stock Research Corporation | www.argusgroup.com |
| WallSt.com | www.wallst.com |
| Wall Street City | www.wallstreetcity.com |
| The Wall Street Journal Interactive Edition | www.wsj.com |
| Wall Street Research Net | www.wsrn.com |
| Zacks Investment Research | www.zacks.com |
| ZDNet | www.zdnet.com |

# The Bottom Line
## Managing Your Portfolio Online

T he appeal of online investing lies in its I-can-do-it-myself attitude. You find a stock, you evaluate it, you enter the buy order. Then you find the next stock, evaluate it, and enter the buy order. Then you do it again and again and again. First thing you know, you have a portfolio of stocks.

Now comes the ultimate do-it-yourself task: managing your portfolio.

Portfolio management is one more step in the investing process that the Internet has lightened and brightened and filled, if not with joy, then with something approaching fun. In the old days, you had to wait for the monthly statement from your stockbroker or read the fine print in newspaper stock tables to track the progress of your holdings. Then came portfolio management software, which computerized the process, for a price—both in terms of dollars and time. Now, along comes the Internet brandishing free portfolio trackers at every other site.

Before we show you what the Web has to offer, let's take a minute to review the process of portfolio management.

## MANAGING A PORTFOLIO

Portfolio management can be broken down into five broad categories:

✔ Monitoring the industry groups represented by your stocks.
✔ Monitoring market conditions.

✔ Allocating your investment dollars among asset groups.

✔ Setting targets and stops for each stock.

✔ Monitoring each stock.

We'll talk about monitoring industry groups and market conditions in Chapter 5. In this chapter we'll show you Internet tools for allocating assets, setting targets and stops, and monitoring your holdings.

## Asset Allocation

The first step in portfolio management is *asset allocation*, which actually should begin before you make your first investment. Asset allocation is a sixty-four-dollar word for determining how you divide your investment dollars among cash, bonds, stocks, mutual funds, and other *asset classes* and subclasses. An ideal allocation is based on your tolerance for risk, your desire for return, and your time horizon.

Several Web sites offer planning tools to help you in this process. Many mutual fund family sites, some bank sites, and a few broker sites offer free financial planning tools, although most are rather simplistic.

The asset allocation planner at Charles Schwab & Co. (www.schwab.com) is fairly typical. (Click Planning at the Schwab home page, then Schwab Answers.) It offers six predetermined plans: short-term, conservative, moderately conservative, moderate, moderately aggressive (shown in Figure 4.1), and aggressive. If you don't know which one best suits you, you can take Schwab's short investor profile questionnaire. If you're a Schwab customer, you can display the current asset allocation of your portfolio, with stocks broken down into large company, small company, international, and other.

Among the more sophisticated planning tools, relatively speaking, is the one at MacroWorld Investor. Now a division of Wachovia Corporation, MacroWorld is a content provider to other Web sites, but it also has its own site at www.mworld.com.

**MacroWorld Forecasts**   MacroWorld is well known for its economic forecasts and probabilities, and applies them to stocks, mutual funds, industries, and the market in general.

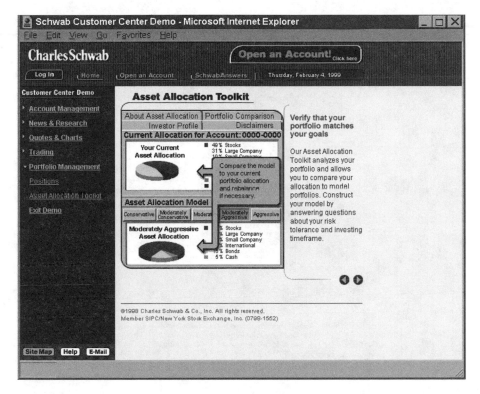

**FIGURE 4.1** The Asset Allocation Toolkit at Charles Schwab & Co. (Reprinted with permission of Charles Schwab & Co., Inc.)

To prepare an investment plan, MacroWorld first establishes your investing profile with a series of screens and a 14-point questionnaire about risk tolerance. Then it provides a multistage analysis, including three options for improving your investment mix (Figure 4.2) and a convenient What If? screen that lets you change any of several values to see the immediate effect on your plan. The MacroWorld site has several free features, but the planning tools are part of its $29/month subscription.

**Other MacroWorld Locations** The MacroWorld tools are available to customers of Security First National Bank at www.sfnb.com and to Level 3 subscribers at Wall Street City.

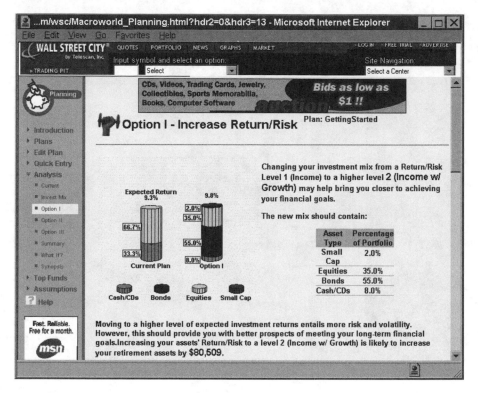

**FIGURE 4.2** The MacroWorld planning tool analyzes your current investment plan and provides three options for changing your investment mix. (Reprinted with permission of Telescan, Inc.)

We encourage you to take advantage of the Web's free planning tools and free trial subscriptions to crystallize your investment goals and discover—if you don't already know it—your attitude toward risk.

**AAII**   The American Association of Individual Investors (www.aaii.com) offers an asset allocation spreadsheet for examining alternatives for balancing risk and return.

In this chapter we will stick to stocks. With regard to stocks, asset allocation simply means spreading your risk among a number of stocks, among different types of stocks, among stocks in different industries, and among stocks bought under different market conditions. Let's take them one at a time.

**Diversify the Number of Stocks** Spreading your risk among a number of stocks is based on common sense. If you put all your eggs in one basket, well, you know the story. The experts don't agree (do they ever?) on how many stocks make up a diversified portfolio. Some say five; some say 20 or more. We side with the latter, simply to increase the margin for error.

A major consideration, however, is the size of your investment nest egg. Like butter, the more money you have, the larger the area you can cover without spreading it too thin. Fifty thousand dollars, for example, can easily accommodate 15 to 20 stocks, for an average investment of about $3000 per stock. On the other hand, trying to buy 20 stocks with just $10,000 would result in about $500 per stock—a very thin spread indeed. In January 1999 that would buy just two shares of Yahoo! or three shares of Microsoft. Common sense will tell you how many stocks to include in your portfolio.

**Market Capitalization** A measure of the size of a company by multiplying the outstanding shares by the price per share; also called market cap.

**Diversify the Market Cap** Stocks with different *market capitalizations* (market cap) react differently to market conditions. Sometimes the large caps or mid caps perform better than small caps or micro caps; sometimes not. Over the past 70 years, small caps have outperformed larger cap stocks, with average returns of two to three points higher. But that has not been the case in the past three to five years; hence, small cap values are very high today—that is, they are undervalued against historical standards.

**Searching by Market Cap** To screen stocks by market cap, enter minimum and maximum values for the market cap criterion, based on the chart in Figure 4.3. For best results, include the average 30-day volume criterion and specify the highest values.

You can play the market cap game two ways: You can put all your money in stocks that represent the leading segment and switch when the tide turns against it. (In the next chapter we'll show you where to find the tools to help you determine the best-performing market caps.) Or you can spread your investment dollars among three or four different segments to reduce your overall risk.

A stock's market capitalization is usually listed on its company profile, and some search programs display it in the search results. Once you know the capitalization, use the chart in Figure 4.3 to see where the stock fits.

**Diversify Industry Groups** When an industry group is hot, as Internet stocks were in late 1998/early 1999, you might wish you'd bet the farm on them. But you would have needed the vision of a Nostradamus and the timing of a con artist to get in and out at the right times. It is far safer to spread the risk among several different industry groups or sectors.

We talk about industry groups at length in Chapter 5, so to avoid repetition we'll refer you to that discussion. Keep in mind that industry group selection is part of the initial stock screening process as well as the ongoing monitoring process.

**Diversify Market Conditions** In a raging bull market, investors often become overly enthusiastic and commit as many dollars as possible in the hope of getting in on the action. This creates more risk because of the inevitability of a *market correction*. It is far wiser to invest on a regular basis, say on the first or fifteenth of every month. This helps to average out the highs and lows at which stocks are acquired and prevents you from committing all your funds at a *market top*. (The mutual fund industry calls this *dollar-cost averaging*.) If you build your portfolio slowly, acquiring two or three stocks a month, you'll automatically diversify the market conditions under which you buy the stocks.

| FIGURE 4.3  Popular Market Cap Classifications | |
| --- | --- |
| *Classification* | *Market Capitalization* |
| Large caps | $3 billion-plus |
| Mid caps | $1 billion to $3 billion |
| Small caps | $300 million to $1 billion |
| Micro caps | Less than $300 million |

**Dollar-Cost Averaging** A system of investing a fixed sum at regular intervals in stocks or mutual funds. Acquiring more shares at lower prices and fewer shares at higher prices helps minimize your market risk.

There is an exception to the rule, of course. If the market is well off its high (*oversold*) and beginning to show upward momentum, you might want to invest more aggressively than normal. (We'll show you how to determine market over- and undervaluation in Chapter 5.)

## Setting Targets and Stops

Monitoring targets and stops is an important part of portfolio management. But first, you have to *set* the target and the stop, and the time to do this is at the time you buy the stock.

**Setting Targets** A target gives you a goal to shoot for. It is the price you think a stock can reasonably reach, given its historical trends, projected earnings, and other factors. A target can be based on a stock's position relative to certain technical indicators, such as *LSQ lines*, *trading bands*, or resistance levels, each of which will suggest a slightly different target. We recommend you use them all and set an average target or a series of targets. We describe how to do this in our *CyberInvesting* book; to recap briefly, the target can be the stock price at the upper trading band, at the resistance line itself, and at the top of the short-term and long-term LSQ channels. The Web tools for plotting these indicators are discussed in Chapter 3.

**LSQ Line** LSQ stands for a mathematical formula called "least squares." In technical analysis, an LSQ line is a trend line that determines the midpoint of price data on a stock graph. An LSQ channel is created by drawing parallel lines on either side of the LSQ line to encompass the trading action.

Another way to arrive at a reasonable target is to use the price target set by the analysts who follow a stock. When analysts announce earnings estimates or a change in their buy/hold/sell recommendations, they usually include the price level they expect the stock to achieve. These are reported as research alerts on several Web sites, including MSN Investor's (www.investor.msn.com) Advisor FYI (see Figure 3.2 in Chapter 3).

**Trading Bands**   On a stock graph, an envelope drawn within a set distance on either side of a moving average to delineate a stock's trading range.

**Targets and LSQ Lines**   The trading channel created by LSQ lines is one of the best ways to set a target. We discuss this at length in our *CyberInvesting* book, but at this writing we are not aware of any Web site that offers LSQ lines as part of its technical arsenal. Technicians will have to revert to offline software for this particular tool.

**Attn: Long-Term Investors**   Long-term investors may not have a specific numerical target, as their goal is to hold the stock as long as the company continues to meet its growth objectives. With that in mind, the long-term investor can check earnings and projections on a quarterly basis. If nothing has changed materially, the stock should be good for another quarter. But even long-term investors will want to reassess a stock that has had a major price drop or bad earnings for more than one quarter.

**Setting Stops**   Setting reasonable stops is one of the marks of a successful investor. A stop is the price at which you intend to sell a stock to limit your losses or protect your profits. Amateur investors tend to neglect this step and end up riding a declining stock far too long. The pros never do.

It is a good idea to set a stop at the time of purchase and adjust it as the stock climbs toward its target. You can use a *hard stop* or a *mental stop*.

A hard stop is an actual stop order that tells your broker to sell the stock should it reach a certain level.

**Setting Stops** An initial stop can be set 10 to 20 percent below the purchase price with subsequent stops set just below an important support level.

We use hard stops sparingly because of their irrevocability. If a stock reaches a hard stop, it is sold automatically. You don't get a chance to change your mind.

A mental stop, on the other hand, is simply a reminder to yourself to reevaluate a stock if it falls to a certain level. A mental stop can be entered in many online portfolio trackers as a price *alert*.

**Stop Orders** If you trade online be sure that your broker allows stop orders, and check whether stop orders on NASDAQ stocks are allowed.

Where should you set a stop? The easiest way is to set it 10 to 20 percent below the purchase price. A more analytical way is to set the stop just below an important support level. You can determine support levels by drawing a horizontal line through a series of stock bottoms (see Figure 3.8 in Chapter 3). As the stock moves up, you should move your stop up as well to protect your profits, keeping it, say, 15 percent below the stock price.

The use of stops is an art, not a science. If you use mental stops, you may want to switch to a hard stop at some point to lock in profits. Although a hard stop doesn't give you a chance to change your mind, it can also prevent hanging on too long in a downtrend.

**Early Warning Alerts** To give yourself time to react, set your targets slightly lower and your mental stops slightly higher than actuals. This will provide an early warning signal to watch the stock closely.

### Monitoring Your Stocks

Web-based portfolio trackers make it easy to keep up with your stocks. They can instantaneously update multiple stock prices, alert you to targets and stops, and provide analysis tools to simplify the monitoring process. Let's look at some of the events that should be monitored; then we'll show you some portfolio trackers on (and off) the Web.

**The Watch List**   You don't have to own stocks to use a portfolio tracker. Set up a watch list to track the progress of stocks in which you're interested.

**Price Alerts** We talked earlier about setting targets and stops for each of your stocks. Monitoring them is a snap with a portfolio tracker that offers price alerts. Simply enter the target as the high price alert and the stop as the low price alert (Figure 4.4). If either price is reached, the Web site will notify you by e-mail or by flagging the stock in the portfolio tracker. (Some Web sites will beep your pager with the price alert.) At that point you can reevaluate the stock to see if it is time to sell.

**News Alerts** Many portfolio trackers will alert you whenever there is a news story about your stock. The alerts can't filter out the important from the trivial, however; they simply include any story in which the company was mentioned. It is up to you to judge the possible impact of the story on the stock. Remember our earlier caveat about "stocks in the news": By the time the news reaches the mass media, its impact is probably already reflected in the stock price.

**E-mail News Alerts**   A word of advice on requesting e-mail news alerts for large company stocks. Don't. You would be inundated with e-mails, because stocks like Microsoft and IBM may appear in dozens of news stories each day. For large stocks, opt for the alert icon on the portfolio tracker.

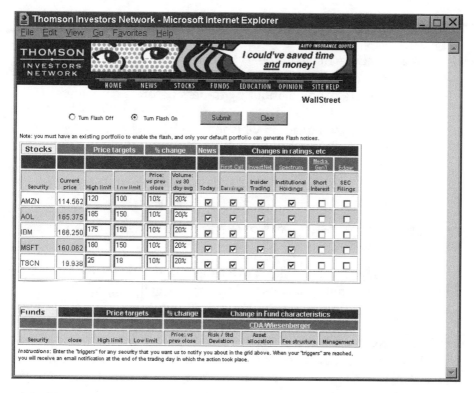

**FIGURE 4.4** The portfolio tracker at Thomson Investors Network allows you to enter price targets and stops, as well as alerts for other events that might affect the stock price. (Reprinted with permission of Thomson Investors Network; © Thomson Investors Network.)

**Earnings Alerts** You should be aware of earnings release dates of the companies in which you own stock. Some online trackers offer special earnings alerts, but if yours doesn't, you might want to check those sites (mentioned later in the chapter) that post schedules of earnings announcements. Be especially watchful for positive earnings surprises, which occur when a company exceeds the analysts' estimates. A positive surprise is a good thing, but keep in mind that the stock price may already reflect the news because of the *whisper numbers* circulated in the market. Nevertheless, if a company meets or exceeds its earnings estimates, you can take it as a positive sign for the future of the stock.

### The Whisper Numbers

A company matches or beats its earnings estimates and the stock price goes down. Why? Whisper numbers. These are numbers bandied about by traders before a company's earnings release, numbers that are based primarily on rumors. To get a bead on whisper numbers, check out EarningsWhispers.com (www.earningswhispers.com). This free site has a calendar of upcoming releases, along with the stock's official earnings estimates and the whisper numbers.

You'll also want to monitor any changes in the analysts' estimates or buy/hold/sell recommendations, which are usually captured in news alerts, often under the heading of Upgrades/Downgrades.

**Insider Trading Alerts** Corporate insiders must file a Form 144 with the SEC each time they buy or sell stock in their own company. The filing must be made within 10 days after the first of the month following the trade. Thus, it is a good idea to check this for each of your stocks once a month. If there is unusually heavy insider selling, you may want to reevaluate the stock to discover the reasons for the selling.

**Technical Alerts** When a stock's technical patterns change, it is a good idea to reassess the stock. A technical alert would be a positive or negative breakout based on one of the popular charting indicators like the MACD or basing patterns. Technical alerts are available from a couple of Web sites, mentioned in the next section. Otherwise, you will need to view a graph of each stock on a daily basis and look for *overbought* conditions or negative breakouts.

**Overbought** A condition that occurs in the market when there are more buyers than sellers and stock prices hover at a precariously high level. An overbought market is ripe for a correction.

Any alert should be considered just that—an alert—not a panic signal to sell. If one of your stocks gives a negative alert, simply go through the same evaluation process as when you bought the stock and see if the negative signal is offset by other conditions. Then decide whether to sell or continue to hold the stock. A positive alert—which could be a positive earnings surprise, heavy insider buying, or an upward revision in earnings estimates—may be a signal to increase your position.

 **Down in a Down Market** If the whole market is down sharply, your stocks probably will be down also. This requires a different kind of assessment, which we talk about in Chapter 5.

Let's move on now to the online resources that make all this monitoring a breeze.

## ONLINE PORTFOLIO TRACKERS

Portfolio trackers have become another one of those freebies that Web sites use to lure you back to their sites. You'll return on a daily basis, they reason, to track the progress of your stocks. Therefore, almost every investing Web site offers some kind of portfolio tracker.

 **Broker Portfolio Trackers** All trades placed online are automatically entered in the free portfolio tracker at the broker's Web site. At this time, most are stripped-down models. Few can be customized and fewer still offer portfolio analysis or sophisticated alerts. This is sure to change for the better in the future.

The portfolio trackers are similar in many ways. Most offer different views that let you see the portfolio's valuation, performance, and fundamental data. Many allow you to customize your own view, taking one column from this view and two columns from that. Most allow you to keep multiple portfolios, so that you can keep a 401(k) portfolio separate from an investment portfolio, a stock portfolio separate from an option or mutual fund portfolio, and a *watch list* separate from the rest. Most have news and price alerts. Most are free, although some of the fancier features carry a premium.

**Watch List**   A list or portfolio of stock prospects that you are watching with an eye for an optimum entry point.

Here are seven of the best portfolio trackers on the Web. All but one are free (the exception is Stock Smart), although some of the free ones have premium features. We recommend that you take a look at all of them to see which best fits your needs.

### MSN Investor

The portfolio tracker at MSN Investor has more bells and whistles than just about any free tracker on the Web. Because it's a Microsoft product, it can take advantage of the familiar Windows 95 tabs, commands, and format that we all know and love (!). Here are a few of our favorite things about the MSN Investor portfolio tracker, shown in Figure 4.5:

✔ *Multiple Views.* The MSN Investor portfolio tracker has at least eight different views—asset allocation, performance, return, calculations, valuation, quotes, holdings, and fundamental data—but the differences among some of the views are subtle. The good news is, you can pick and choose from an array of 40 pieces of data to create a customized view. This is the only portfolio tracker we found that allows you to enter a comment about a stock.

✔ *Advisor FYI Alerts.* MSN Investor has the standard price alerts, e-mailed if you wish, but its news alerts are part of the Advisor FYI, which we mentioned briefly in Chapter 3. More than 20 different events will trigger an FYI alert, noted by the FYI icon next to the stock in your portfolio. Among the triggers are analyst projections, SEC filings, changes in key balance sheet ratios and figures, mention of the stock in one of MSN Investor's columns or editorials, and the stock turning up in one of its

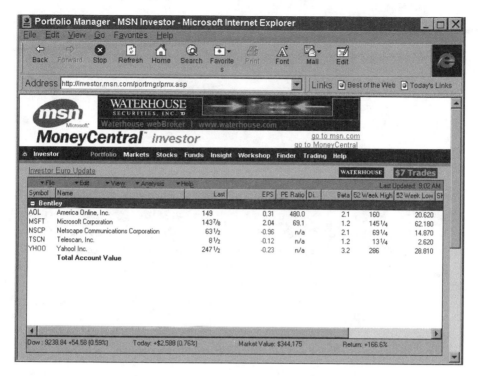

**FIGURE 4.5** A fundamental data view of a portfolio at MSN Investor. (Reprinted with permission of Microsoft Corporation.)

fund or stock screens. It also includes technical alerts, such as crossovers of the 200-day or 50-day moving average, a change in institutional ownership, a price move on heavy volume, and a change in relative strength. The portfolio tracker itself is free, but the price alerts and Advisor FYI are part of the $9.95 site subscription.

✔ *Importing/Exporting Data.* Perhaps the biggest advantage of an MSN Investor portfolio tracker is its ability to transfer data both online and offline. Portfolios can be imported from many online brokers, so that you don't have to reenter each transaction when you make a trade. You can also import data from and export data to Microsoft Money 99 and Quicken 99, as well as export it in a spreadsheet format suitable for other software. This is important because no Web-based portfolio tracker offers substantial tax-reporting features at this time.

**Microsoft Money 99 and Quicken 99**   These are two of the most popular offline money management programs, both of which offer investment portfolios and online access to their respective Web sites (where you can order the products online). Each costs about $60 each, less $20 for updates.

## Reuters Moneynet

You'll find a good free portfolio tracker at this Reuters Web site (www.moneynet.com). A *drop-down menu* offers several different views of the portfolio. The Quotes view provides links to news, *intraday charts*, price history, detailed quotes, company profiles, and research. A Custom view lets you decide which data to display. There's also a P&L bar graph and a distribution pie chart. A unique feature of the Moneynet portfolio tracker is the ability to track valuations in more than 30 currencies.

**Intraday Chart**   A price-and-volume stock chart that tracks the minute-by-minute trades during the day.

## Morningstar.Net

Morningstar.Net (www.morningstar.net) has a great portfolio tracker, especially if mutual funds are part of your holdings. With its Portfolio X-Ray feature, you can monitor your portfolio to see:

**1.** Whether the stocks are over- or undervalued (Stock Stats X-Ray).

**2.** The allocation of stocks and/or mutual funds among major asset classes (Asset Class X-Ray—Figure 4.6), among stock sectors (Stock Sector X-Ray), among global assets (World Regions X-Ray), and among bonds (Bond Style X-Ray).

**3.** How much you're paying mutual fund managers for fees and expenses (Fees & Expenses X-Ray).

The Stock Stats, Asset Class, and Fees & Expenses X-Rays are free; the others are part of the $9.95/month site subscription.

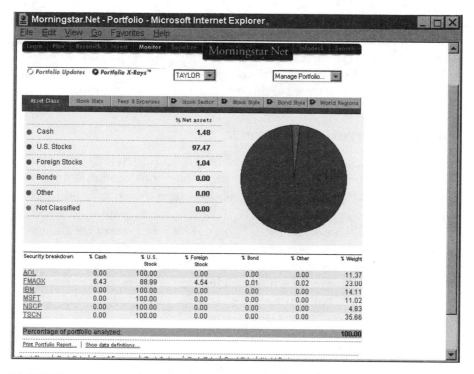

**FIGURE 4.6** Morningstar.Net's Asset Class X-Ray shows a portfolio's allocation among cash, bonds, U.S. stocks, and foreign stocks. (Reprinted with permission of Morningstar, Inc.)

## Quicken.com

Quicken.com's portfolio tracker (www.quicken.com/investments) can transfer data to the offline Quicken for Windows program and, via that program, to various broker accounts. But the online tracker itself is no slouch. You can customize the portfolio view by selecting from more than 30 pieces of data, and analyze the portfolio composition with asset allocation pie charts. There is also a cool Stock Evaluator that compares the stocks graphically (in a bar chart) on 11 fundamental factors. Quicken is generous with alerts, which include price percentage change, upgrades/downgrades, stock splits, volume, and earnings and dividend announcements.

## Stock Smart

Stock Smart's portfolio tracker is not free, but if you're subscribing to the site (located at www.stocksmart.com) for other reasons, the tracker is a nice bonus. Noteworthy features include cash accounts, downloading portfolio data into a spreadsheet, profit and loss statements for closed positions using the FIFO (first in, first out) method, automatic adjustment for splits and symbol changes, and e-mail/pager alerts (these cost $5.95 over and above the $12.95 site subscription). There is a good portfolio tutorial.

## Thompson Investors Network

The portfolio tracker at Thomson Investors Network (www.thomsoninvest. net) allows you to track long and short positions, commissions, and closed positions for assessing tax liability. It automatically adjusts for splits and can be converted to a live ticker. The best feature, however, is the alert system. Price alerts include high, low, and percentage change in price and volume; news alerts include today's news and changes in earnings estimates, insider trading, institutional holdings, short interest, and SEC filings. Alerts for mutual funds include price alerts, plus changes in a fund's risk level, asset allocation, fee structure, and management.

## Wall Street City

The portfolio tracker at Wall Street City (www.wallstreetcity.com) looks like all the others at first glance, but there are one-of-a-kind reports and technical breakout alerts you won't find anywhere else (all subscription-based). In addition to the Telescan Rankings described in Chapter 3, there are three additional reports worth a look, plus pager alerts:

- ✔ *The Analysts Ratings.* This report shows the average rating of all analysts who follow a stock. For each stock the average rating is shown on a continuum from strong sell to strong buy. There is also a cumulative rank for the portfolio.
- ✔ *Portfolio Insider Trading.* This report (Figure 4.7) scans the portfolio for insider buying or selling and displays the number of buys and sells, along with an overall ranking of each stock and the entire portfolio.
- ✔ *The MacroWorld Price Forecasts.* This report uses the MacroWorld proprietary stock price forecasting system to forecast the one-day to four-month gain (or loss) for each stock.
- ✔ *Pager Alerts.* With a product called Telescan Direct, Wall Street City will beep your pager with price, volume, news, and technical alerts. The service is not cheap and the pricing is somewhat com-

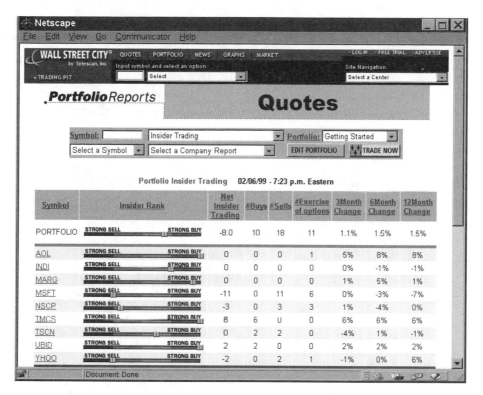

**FIGURE 4.7** Wall Street City's Portfolio Insider Trading report ranks your entire portfolio and each stock individually for heavy insider buying and selling. (Reprinted with permission of Telescan, Inc.)

plex (depending on whether you want real-time or delayed quotes and news and whether you subscribe to any other Wall Street City services), but technicians will love it.

## SUMMARY

Keeping track of what you own is the most important part of investing. Short-term investors will monitor their stocks on a daily or weekly basis. Long-term investors will do it monthly or quarterly. But if you are an on-line investor, we'll bet good money you can't resist checking your positions every day or so just because you can.

One last thought about portfolio performance. To judge it objectively, you need to compare it quarterly with a market index or mutual fund that mimics the portfolio's composition. There is a handy table at the Mutual Fund Investor's Center (see Figure 7.3 in Chapter 7) that seems designed for this purpose. Don't rush to judgment, however, if the index or fund is outperforming your portfolio. But if you're lagging behind for two consecutive quarters, you might want to review your stocks for sell opportunities or industry group rotation. The latter, as it happens, is coming up in the next chapter.

## WEB SITES FOR MANAGING YOUR PORTFOLIO

| | |
|---|---|
| American Association of Individual Investors | www.aaii.com |
| EarningsWhispers.com | www.earningswhispers.com |
| MacroWorld Investor | www.mworld.com |
| Morningstar.Net | www.morningstar.net |
| MSN Investor | www.investor.msn.com |
| Quicken.com | www.quicken.com/investments |
| Reuters Moneynet | www.moneynet.com |
| Charles Schwab & Co. | www.schwab.com |
| Security First National Bank | www.sfnb.com |
| Stock Smart | www.stocksmart.com |
| Thomson Investors Network | www.thomsoninvest.net |
| Wall Street City | www.wallstreetcity.com |

# Bulls versus Bears
## Keeping Up with the Market

O n July 17, 1998, the Dow broke 9300 for the first time. Less than six weeks later it had dropped 1800 points, losing 588 points on August 28 in the biggest one-day point drop ever. "What's the market doing?" became the hottest question of the day, and during the period that followed, online investors were getting a lot of their answers from the Internet.

Whether the Internet contributed to the market's extreme volatility is debatable. It has been said, however, that the easy access to market information makes small investors more likely to react to market ups and downs than in the old days.

Whatever the case, the market goes up and the market goes down. It always has and it always will. As an online investor, you now have a ringside seat on the Internet and yours is one of the hands on the bell.

Monitoring the market is part of the portfolio management process, but how closely you watch it depends to some extent on whether you are a short-term or a long-term investor. Short-term investors try to time their entry and exit points to take advantage of market conditions; long-term investors are relatively unconcerned about the market's daily movements.

Whichever you are, you need to know what, exactly, you are monitoring when you monitor "the market." Even though we use the terms *bull market* and *bear market* to describe the market as a whole, the market is not a single-celled organism. It is made up of different segments—market indexes—that often move independently of each other. Let's take a minute to examine a few of the most popular *market indexes* that we use to talk about the market.

**Cashing Out in Extended Markets**   When the market becomes extended (dangerously high), it can be a signal even to long-term investors that maybe it's time to cash out a portion of their holdings. Not only does this offer protection, it provides cash to buy undervalued stocks when the market bottoms out. An overly extended market is one that is well above a long-term trend line connecting past peaks.

## MARKET INDEXES

The most common market indexes are the Dow, the NASDAQ, the New York Stock Exchange, the S&P 500, and the S&P 100.

### The Dow

The market index that is most synonymous with "the market" is the *Dow Jones Industrial Average (the Dow)* (Figure 5.1). When we say the market fell 588 points on August 28, 1998, it was the Dow that fell 588 points. The drop was significant in terms of percentage (it was a 6.8 percent drop from the total value of the index). The Dow itself is less significant when you consider that it is made up of only 30 stocks that represent the largest companies in America.

**The Dow Companies**   A list of the companies that make up the Dow can be found at the Bloomberg Web site (www.bloomberg.com).

While the Dow is the best-known barometer of the market, it is much too narrow for analyzing the market as a whole. For that, you need the broader indexes like the NASDAQ, the New York Stock Exchange (NYSE) composite index, and the S&P 500.

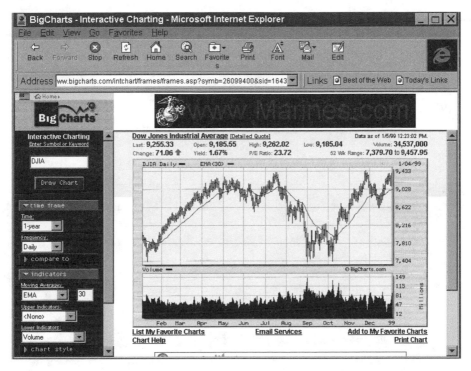

**FIGURE 5.1** This one-year graph of the Dow Jones Industrial Average shows its precipitous decline in late summer 1998 and the subsequent recovery. (Reprinted with permission of BigCharts, Inc.)

## The NASDAQ Composite Index

The NASDAQ stock market is an electronic market comprising more than 5000 companies, including leading-edge growth companies and many smaller cap companies. Because of its heavy concentration of high-technology companies, it is considered a barometer of technology stocks.

**NASD and OTC** NASDAQ is regulated by the National Association of Securities Dealers (www.nasd.com). NASDAQ is also referred to as the over-the-counter (OTC) market because trades are made "over the counter"—or more accurately, over the computer—rather than on the floor of an exchange.

   The NASDAQ is a two-tiered structure. The NASDAQ National Market is comprised of larger companies with the most actively traded securities; the NASDAQ Small-Cap Market is made up, in general, of companies with assets of less than $12 million. Within these two tiers, there are more than a dozen NASDAQ indexes; the one most often quoted as "the NASDAQ" is the NASDAQ OTC Composite Index (Figure 5.2), which comprises all 5400 stocks. You can find out more about the NASDAQ at www.nasdaq.com.

**NASDAQ versus the Dow**   The NASDAQ index is valued at about one-fifth of the Dow; therefore, a one-point change in the NASDAQ is equivalent to a five-point change in the Dow.

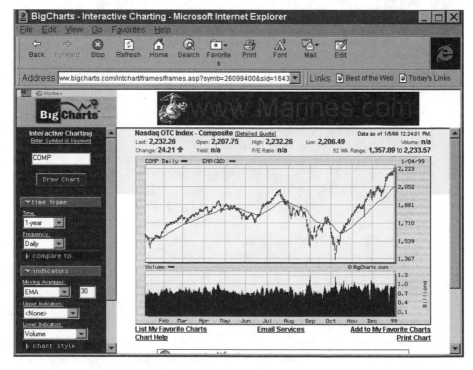

**FIGURE 5.2**   The NASDAQ OTC Composite Index tracked the Dow's decline and recovery. (Reprinted with permission of BigCharts, Inc.)

### The New York Stock Exchange Composite Index

The New York Stock Exchange (NYSE) composite index is made up of all 3300 stocks listed on the New York Stock Exchange. The index is weighted for capitalization, as are the NASDAQ and the S&P 500. This means that activity in the larger-cap stocks will move the index more than similar activity in the mid-cap stocks. There is, by the way, an interesting history of the NYSE at its Web site (www.nyse.com).

**Links to Company Web Sites**   Both the NYSE and the NASDAQ have links to the Web sites of their listed companies.

### The S&P 500 and S&P 100

Standard & Poor's created two indexes that have become bellwethers of the market. The S&P 500 (Figure 5.3) is made up of 500 large- and mid-cap stocks representing all major industries. It was designed to represent the broad domestic economy. The S&P 100, also known as the *OEX*, contains the 100 largest stocks from the S&P 500. (If you're partial to large, well-established companies, the OEX would be a good benchmark for your portfolio.)

**OEX**   A commonly traded index option based on the S&P 100.

These indexes—the Dow, the NASDAQ, the NYSE, the S&P 500, and the S&P 100—are the most widely quoted indicators of market activity. They're the market stats you'll see on most Web sites.

### Other Indexes

There are several other indexes you might want to be aware of.

✔ *The American Stock Exchange (AMEX).* The AMEX is composed of about 900 companies representing many different industries.

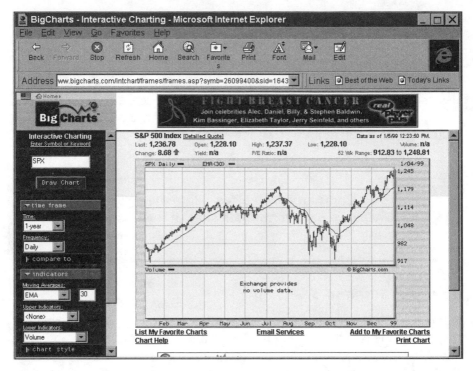

**FIGURE 5.3** This one-year graph for the S&P 500 shows its participation in the market plunge in late summer 1998. (Reprinted with permission of BigCharts, Inc.)

(It is also a primary marketplace for *derivative securities*.) The AMEX (www.amex.com) has been known as the place for smaller companies that can't attract sufficient following by NASDAQ *market makers*. In October 1998, the AMEX became a part of NASDAQ.

---

 **Derivative Security**    A security whose value is based on (derived from) another (underlying) security, such a stock or market index. Options and futures are derivatives.

**Market Maker**   A firm that "makes a market" in an over-the-counter (NASDAQ) security by maintaining a firm bid and offer price.

✔ *The Russell Indexes.* These were created by the Frank Russell Company for stocks in the United States, Australia, Canada, and Japan. The most widely quoted Russell index is the Russell 2000, which is made up of 2000 small-cap stocks (with an average market cap of $592 million). Descriptions of the Russell indexes can be found at www.russell.com.

✔ *Internet and Technology Indexes.* NASDAQ is not the only barometer of technology stocks. Red Herring Online (www.redherring.com) has the Tech 250 Composite, the Tech 250 Communications, the Tech 250 Computers, and the Tech 250 Entertainment indexes. The Internet Stock Index (ISDEX at http://fast.quote.com/groups/isdex.html) tracks 50 of the largest and most active Internet stocks (Figure 5.4). The @Net and the @100 are Internet stock indexes created by ZDNet (www.zdnet.com). ZDNet also has a global technology index that combines the performance of 30 Asian, 30 European, and 40 North American companies.

✔ *The INDI SmallCap 500 Index.* This is a new market index from Individual Investor Online (www.iionline.com). Listed on the American Stock Exchange (ticker symbol NDI), it is comprised of smaller cap companies with rapid earnings growth.

## TECHNICAL SNAPSHOTS OF MARKET INDEXES

Market indexes can be analyzed from a technical standpoint, just like stocks. Two simple trend lines can give you a quick insight into the market's technical patterns. One is a horizontal support line; the other is a diagonal support line to mark a long-term trend. A falling market is likely to get support at these crucial levels and bottom out; if that doesn't happen, it is likely to continue to fall to the next major support level.

---

ISDEX (Internet Stock Index) -- the Pure Play... - Microsoft Internet Explorer    _ □ ✕

File   Edit   View   Go   Favorites   Help

**isdex** internet stock index   stock quotes provided by ⊕ QUOTE.COM

The Current ISDEX value is 274.85 with a change of -23.13 (-7.76%)

| Tuesday, January 5, 12:25 PM Eastern time | | | | | | |
|---|---|---|---|---|---|---|
| Company | Stock Symbol | Time | Last | Change | Volume | Business |
| @Home | ATHM | 12:10 | 78 1/16 | -15/16 | 772,200 | Cable Internet services |
| 24/7 | TFSM | 12:08 | 28 3/8 | +1 3/8 | 61,900 | Ad network |
| Amazon | AMZN | 12:10 | 127 3/4 | +9 7/16 | 21,395,400 | E-tailer of books, music, video |
| AOL | AOL | 12:05 | 149 1/8 | +5/16 | 7,097,500 | Consumer online services |
| Axent | AXNT | 12:07 | 30 | -1/16 | 115,300 | Web security software |
| Beyond.com | BYND | 12:05 | 22 3/4 | +15/16 | 340,700 | Software Retailer Network |
| Broadcast.com | BCST | 12:08 | 79 1/4 | -3 5/16 | 76,100 | Web audio-video aggregator |
| Broadcom | BRCM | 12:10 | 132 | +5 1/8 | 283,000 | Broadband chips |
| Broadvision | BVSN | 12:05 | 33 1/2 | -1/8 | 136,000 | Web marketing software |
| CDnow | CDNW | 12:09 | 18 15/16 | +1/16 | 408,900 | E-tailer for music |
| CheckPoint Software | CHKPF | 12:10 | 45 1/2 | +2 5/16 | 444,200 | Web security software |
| Cisco | CSCO | 12:10 | 96 5/16 | +1 | 5,862,100 | Leading Internet routing firm |
| CKS Group | CKSG | N/A | N/A | N/A | N/A | Web marketing services |
| CMG Info | CMGI | 12:10 | 112 11/16 | -1 13/16 | 391,400 | Internet venture firm |
| CNET | CNWK | N/A | N/A | N/A | N/A | Web and cable content |
| Concentric | CNCX | 12:06 | 32 1/4 | -3/8 | 36,100 | Internet services provider |
| Cybercash | CYCH | 12:08 | 15 3/8 | -1/8 | 156,000 | Digital currencies |

**FIGURE 5.4**   The ISDEX tracks 50 of the most prominent Internet stocks. (Source: Originally appeared on Mecklermedia Corporation's www.internet.com Web site. Copyright © 1998 Mecklermedia Corporation, 20 Ketchum Street, Westport, CT 06880. All rights reserved. Reprinted with permission.)

---

**Drawing Support Lines**   Support lines should be drawn through market bottoms, either horizontally or diagonally. The more bottoms that the line touches, the stronger the support at that level.

---

During 1998, the NASDAQ's primary support level was about 1700, but in late August it plunged all the way to the secondary support level of 1500. Over the next month, it recovered and again pushed through the 1700 level, only to plummet again in early October to the crucial 1500 level.

Support lines and trend lines are the equivalent of a simple black-

and-white snapshot of the market. For a more sophisticated *technical* analysis see the market commentary at PersonalWealth.com, Wall Street City, or any of the market timing newsletters, described later in this chapter.

Let's look now at what the Web has to offer in the way of monitoring the market from a news and commentary standpoint.

## MARKET MONITOR SITES

There are five major news sites that can help you stay on top of the market: Bloomberg, Briefing.com, CBS MarketWatch, TheStreet.com, and the Wall Street Journal/Barron's. They all have market stats, market news, and original market commentary. The differences lie mainly in their styles.

### Bloomberg

Bloomberg was the reigning pre-Internet disseminator of market data via its *Bloomberg terminal*, which sat on the desks of thousands of professional investors. The Bloomberg Web site (www.bloomberg.com) doesn't pretend to duplicate its terminals, but it is loaded with (mostly free) market stats. On the home page, for example, you'll find stats for equity indexes, interest rates, mortgage rates, commodities, and currencies, each linked to its own page of dozens more stats. Figure 5.5 shows the Bloomberg Markets page that leads to even more stats.

Bloomberg offers some stats we haven't seen elsewhere: performance figures for each of the 30 Dow stocks and each of the S&P 500 stocks. There are also a couple dozen daily and weekly columns on the market and finance. All this is free, but certain features, such as the portfolio tracker, online stock quotes, company news, and mutual funds, are reserved for subscribers of the *Bloomberg Personal Finance* magazine (at $24.95/year).

### Briefing.com

A favorite of *Business Week*, *Barron's*, and Dow Jones, Briefing.com (www.briefing.com) is short on graphics and long on solid market information. There are a few freebies: the market snapshot (Figure 5.6), intraday market commentary, quotes and charts, portfolio trackers, sector ratings, and an economic calendar.

All else is divided among two subscription levels. The Stock Analysis

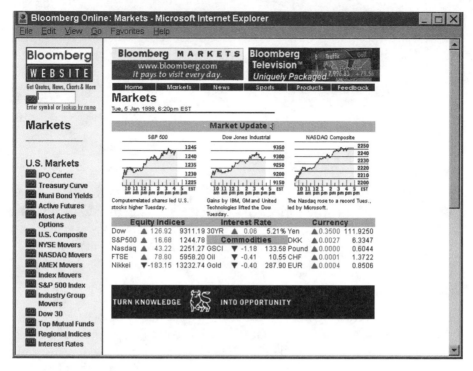

**FIGURE 5.5** The Markets page at Bloomberg. (Source: Bloomberg. Reprinted with permission.)

subscription ($6.95/month) includes constantly updated market analysis and other market news. The Professional subscription ($25/month) provides in-depth coverage of the fixed income and foreign exchange (FX) markets, live bond market commentary, and rapid analysis of economic releases.

## CBS MarketWatch

CBS MarketWatch (cbs.marketwatch.com/news/newsroom.htx) is a free site packed with market news updated throughout the day (Figure 5.7). More than three dozen columns offer commentary and opinions by market experts. (A helpful link describes the focus and writer of each column.) Plus, you'll find an earnings release calendar, analysts' upgrades and downgrades, the latest stock splits and corporate buybacks, and a calendar of economic reports along with their forecasted numbers and comparison figures. For the really active trader who watches every tick of the market, CBS MarketWatch offers real-time, continuous, live equity quotes and news for $79 a month.

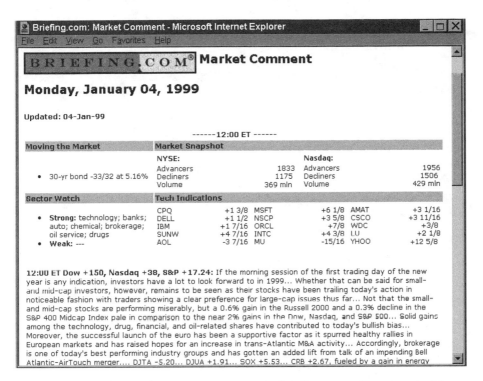

**FIGURE 5.6** The Market Comment page at Briefing.com. (Reprinted with permission of Briefing.com.)

**Real-Time, Continuous, Live Equity Quotes** Quotes that include the most recent trade and are automatically updated, tick by tick, with each new trade.

## TheStreet.com

If you want your market commentary with attitude, try TheStreet.com (www.thestreet.com—Figure 5.8). This popular new media site is loaded with well-written market commentary, including the in-your-face opinions of head Streeter James J. Cramer. The market update and some of the tools are free, but the commentary and opinions cost $6.95/month, or $9.95 if you want the daily e-mail bulletin.

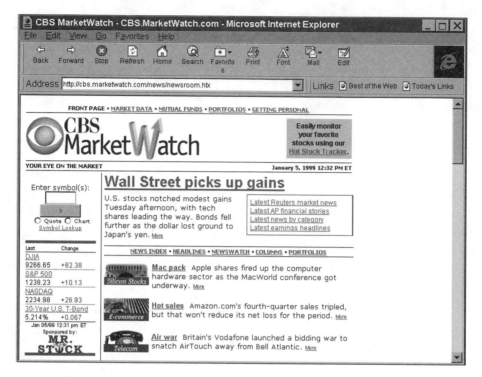

**FIGURE 5.7**  The home page of CBS MarketWatch. (Reprinted with permission of CBS MarketWatch.)

## WSJ.com and Barron's Online

Fans of the *Wall Street Journal* will love having the online edition at their fingertips. The Wall Street Journal Interactive Edition has the same look and feel as the print *Journal*, with similar sections, such as the Money & Investing page and dozens of columns and opinions from top market experts. A "Heard on the Net" column is modeled after its "Heard on the Street" column, which is also available online.

With a subscription to the Interactive Journal, you also get Barron's Online. It is basically an electronic version of the weekly print publication, with two exceptions: an online supplement called the Weekday Extra, which offers special columns and articles for online subscribers, and a daily e-mail called the Weekday Trader, which analyzes a different stock or industry (this is a good prospecting tool!).

**FIGURE 5.8** The home page of TheStreet.com. (Reprinted with permission of TheStreet.com.)

## Other News Sites

All the major news media have online counterparts. Here are some you might want to check out:

ABC News (www.abcnews.com)

Business Week (www.businessweek.com)

CNBC (www.cnbc.com)

CNNfn (www.cnnfn.com—Figure 5.9)

Forbes (www.forbes.com)

Fortune.com (www.fortune.com)

Fox News (www.foxnews.com)

The Internet Stock Report (www.internetnews.com/stocks) Great coverage of Internet stocks.

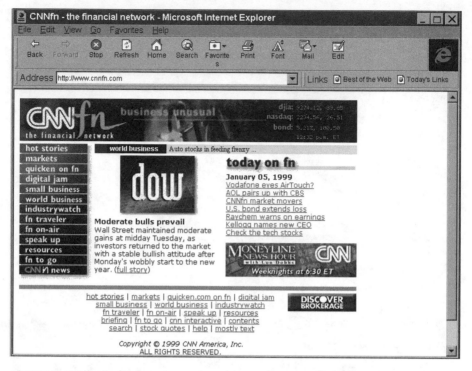

**FIGURE 5.9** The home page of CNNfn. (Copyright © 1999 Time Inc. New Media. All rights reserved. Reproduction in whole or in part without permission is prohibited. Pathfinder is a registered trademark of Time Inc. New Media.)

Money Talks (www.talks.com) Good weekly market commentary columns.

MSNBC (www.msnbc.com)

News.com (from CNET—www.news.com)

The New York Times (www.nytimes.com)

USA Today (www.usatoday.com)

ZDNet (www.zdnet.com)

## Customized News Pages

If you don't want to surf the Net to find the latest news, you can customize your own news page. Customization is a big trend on the Net. The sites shown below allow you to select news categories and specific companies that you wish to follow. Other sites will no doubt follow suit.

Custom News at CNNfn (www.cnnfn.com)

Custom News at News.com (www.news.com)

My Newspage (www.newspage.com)

My Snap! (www.snap.com)

My Yahoo! (www.yahoo.com)

The Wall Street Journal's Personal Edition (www.wsj.com)

# MARKET MONITORS AT INVESTING SUPERSITES

Market updates and market news are so readily available that investing supersites have had to become very creative to compete with dedicated news sites. Here are several supersites with market commentary or news worth checking out.

## MSN Investor

MSN Investor (investor.msn.com) gets its market report from the Wall Street Journal Interactive Edition five times a day. It also has business headlines from MSNBC and news categorized by industry or topic (research alerts, earnings forecasts, earnings results, mergers and acquisitions, initial public offerings, U.S. Treasuries, and economic indicators)—all part of the $9.95/month subscription.

## The Motley Fool

For those who enjoy the irreverent style of The Motley Fool (www.fool.com), there is a morning report (Breakfast News), midday analysis (Lunchtime News), and evening wrap-up (Evening News). These are free on-site, but $39/year for e-mail delivery.

## PersonalWealth.com

This S&P site (www.personalwealth.com) has a robust market monitor/news section. There are original commentary and analysis, a monthly and quarterly market outlook, and a look at the market from a technical perspective. Other features like Word on the Street, Analysts' Picks & Pans, and MarketMovers offer quick takes on various equities. If you have a *RealAudio* player, you can listen to the S&P analysts' conference call first thing in the morning. Some of these features are free; others are part of the $9.95/month subscription.

**RealAudio**    Downloadable software that improves the sound quality on your computer and enables you to enjoy the audio features of many Web sites; available at www.realaudio.com.

### Wall Street City

Wall Street City (www.wallstreetcity.com) has a free, three-times-daily market commentary, plus a dozen or so informative daily columns in its newly revised market section. Two of the columns are aimed at traders and short-term investors. The Trader analyzes the market through various technical lenses, and the BBR (Brown Breakout Ratio, a proprietary market timing indicator) alerts viewers to short-term technical trends. There is also a free section called Market Consensus that summarizes the opinions and forecasts of well-known market experts.

### Local Market Coverage

If you're interested in your local economy or just want to know how your city is doing in the market as a whole, check out this local market coverage.

- ✔ Quote.com (www.quote.com) has built 40 city or regional indexes that let you track the public companies in a particular city or region (see Figure 5.10). There are also links to the top local business stories. You'll find both in the CityWatch section.

- ✔ American City Business Journals (www.amcity.com) summarizes headlines from 39 city business journals with links to each journal's home page. In addition, American City publishes online reports on six industries: health care, high tech, banking and

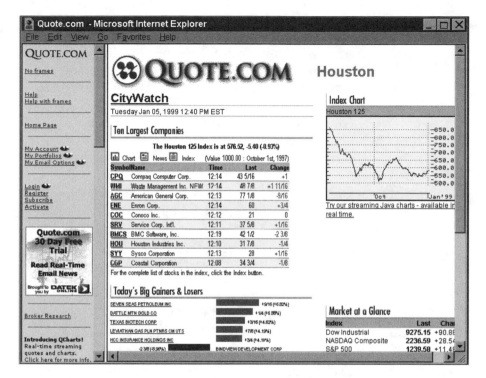

**FIGURE 5.10** The CityWatch page for Houston, Texas, at Quote.com. (Reprinted with permission of Quote.com.)

finance, tourism and hospitality, and retailing/restaurants. You can search the reports by city.

## Investment Newsletters

If you want to pay market experts for advice and commentary, you'll find hundreds of their investment newsletters on the Web. Many have their own Web sites, which you'll find through banner ads and links from other sites; others are clustered on a single site.

Four of the main aggregation sites are The Financial Center (www.tfc.com), Fination.com (www.fination.com), INVESTools (www.investools.com), and Wall Street City (www.wallstreetcity.com). Each has free samples and special offers. For example, the free Market Mavens Report (Figure 5.11) gives you the flavor of many different newsletters. INVESTools features a digest of some of its newsletter offerings under Today's Advisory.

**Rating the Experts**   Mark Hulbert, editor of the Hulbert Financial Digest (www.hulbertdigest.com) is well known for his ratings of more than 160 investment newsletters. This is a subscription site, but you can get the annual Forbes/Hulbert Investment Letter Survey free at the Forbes site (www.forbes.com). Of the 59 investment letters rated in January 1998, only 5 qualified for the Forbes/Hulbert honor roll: Jack Bower's Fidelity Monitor, Paul A. Merriman's Fund Exchange, Gregory Weiss's Investment Quality Trends, Peter Dag's Portfolio Strategy & Management, and Gerald Appel's Systems and Forecasts.

**FIGURE 5.11**   The Market Mavens Report is published at The Financial Center and MarketMavensReport.com. (Reprinted with permission of Pinson Communications, Inc.)

## INDUSTRY GROUP ROTATION

Swimming with the tide is easier than swimming against it. That's why it is important to pay attention to industry group performance. As John Bollinger, developer of the Bollinger bands, says: "A strong stock in a strong group is going to outperform a strong stock in a weak group."

Strong groups and weak groups are the result of the shifting focus of institutional investors. The movement of different industries or sectors into and out of institutional favor creates upward and downward trends. This movement is called *industry group rotation.*

The primary cause of industry group rotation is the intense buying or selling pressure on the stocks within a group or sector. A group may move into favor because some economic indicator points toward increased profits in the group, and vice versa: A group may move out of favor because a negative event or economic indicator points toward a drop in profits for that group. For example, a drop in housing starts is bad for industries such as home appliances or building materials. A decrease in interest rates is good for the housing industry; a decrease in oil prices is good for airlines. Increases in these indicators have the opposite effect.

*Institutional investors* tend to follow one another like lemmings into the favored group, and when they focus on a group, the best stocks in the group benefit from the impact of institutional dollars. The astute individual investor can benefit by following the big guys' lead. Here's how.

When money managers of mutual funds or pension funds find a stock in an industry they like, their usual objective is to acquire a substantial number—usually hundreds of thousands—of shares. To avoid pushing up the price, they must buy shares over a period of time, and this presents a great opportunity for individual investors.

With a buy order of a few hundred or few thousand shares, small investors can move in and out of the market quickly. The general idea is to identify industries favored by the institutions and pick a stock in a group according to your investing philosophy. For example, momentum investors will pick the hottest stock in the group while value investors will opt for undervalued stocks that have not yet participated in the trend. Then, while institutions are accumulating their positions, these investors can ride the upward trend created by the flow of institutional dollars.

This is part of the stock prospecting and research process described earlier. Once you've bought the stock, you'll need to keep an eye on the group to see if and when it begins to lose institutional favor. How? By watching the group the same way you watch a stock, using technical analysis tools to chart the trend. Some examples of weakness: the MACD going negative; a break of an upward trend line; general weakness compared with the market. These can be signals that a downward rotation is about to begin.

Industry group rotation is not quite this clear-cut, but there are online tools that can help you distinguish the rising stars from the falling stars. The tools include independent reports and news on various industries, performance figures (industry stats), industry group graphs, and industry screens. Let's look at a few sites that focus on sectors and industries.

## PersonalWealth.com

The industry section of PersonalWealth.com (www.personalwealth.com) contains a wealth of data. To get there, click the News/Research tab on the home page. Then, select an industry to get to the following:

- ✔ A report from S&P analysts along with a five-year chart.
- ✔ The latest news about companies in the industry.
- ✔ Performance figures for the industry leaders.
- ✔ S&P's "picks and pans"—stocks in the industry group that carry the S&P one- to five-star ratings.

In addition, an Industry in Focus page reports on the hottest industries, and a Sector Scorecard presents the one-month and year-to-date price changes for sectors and industries. Surprisingly, S&P does not offer industry graphs on demand—just the preset five-year graph on the industry report.

## Wall Street City

Performance figures are one thing, but to see the long-term pattern of an industry group, you need a historical graph. One of the few places on the Net to plot industry group graphs with variable time frames is Wall Street City (www.wallstreetcity.com).

To plot a graph, click Industry Group Center, then Best & Worst Industries. This displays a performance bar chart for all 200-plus industry groups (Figure 5.12). Click on a bar to see a list of stocks in that group (ranked by performance); then select the group name and Graph—Industry from the *pull-down menus* to plot a one-year graph for that group. Once a

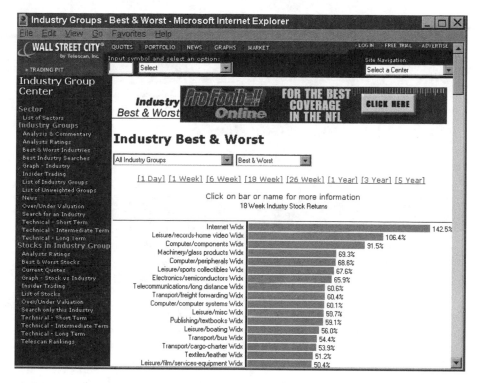

**FIGURE 5.12** The Best & Worst Industries chart at Wall Street City. (Reprinted with permission of Telescan, Inc.)

graph is displayed, you can change the time frame to view the long-term performance. Other features worth exploring here are Analysis & Commentary and Search for an Industry.

## And Consider These . . .

Here are other sites with good industry group features:

✔ *SmartMoney.com's* Sector Tracker (www.smartmoney.com) displays the leading and lagging sectors of the market (Figure 5.13). A drop-down menu takes you to industry gainers and losers, plus the performance (one day to 52 weeks) of industries within each of 11 sectors.

✔ *Individual Investor Online* (www.iionline.com) regularly analyzes eight major industries (automotive, biotech, computers, energy,

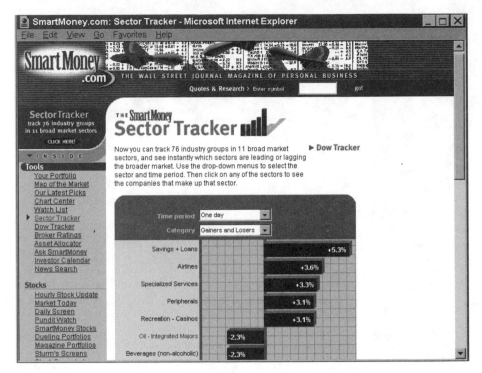

**FIGURE 5.13** The Sector Tracker at SmartMoney.com tracks the performance of market sectors and industry groups. (Reprinted with permission of SmartMoney.com. © 1996–1999 SmartMoney. SmartMoney is a joint publishing venture of Dow Jones & Company, Inc. and The Hearst Corporation.)

finance, Internet, semiconductors, and telecommunications). Be sure to check out the archives.

✔ *Market Guide Investor* (www.marketguide.com) offers its What's Hot/What's Not section, mentioned earlier, for daily performance figures on the best and worst sectors and industries.

✔ *CBS MarketWatch* (cbs.marketwatch.com) has a list of performance figures for about 57 industry group indexes. Click an index symbol to pull up a fixed-term (six-month) graph; click the index name to see a list of stocks in the group.

✔ *StreetNet* (www.streetnet.com) features analytical reports on selected industries.

✔ *MSN Investor* (investor.msn.com) and *StockSite* (www.stocksite.com) both offer news categorized by industries.

# MONITORING ECONOMIC REPORTS

Ever hear of the Beige Book? The Johnson Redbook? The Atlanta Fed Index? The Michigan Sentiment? These and other leading economic indicators can move the market when the latest report is released by the government. The astute investor will know the significance of the reports, the release dates, and the expected effect on the market. Several sites offer economic calendars, but the following give you a little extra:

- ✔ Briefing.com's free Market Calendar (www.briefing.com) gives the release date for each report, Briefing.com's forecast, the market's consensus estimate, the prior figures, and the actual figures as they are released.

- ✔ For an analysis of the important reports as they're released, try the Economic Brief at PersonalWealth.com (www.personalwealth. com). There's much more in the Economy section, most of which is part of the $9.95 site subscription.

- ✔ For a weekly analysis of the U.S. economy, go to StockSite at www.stocksite.com.

# SUMMARY

Market monitoring is an unavoidable part of investing. But don't become too enamored of the market's day-to-day movement (unless you do day trading). (In a volatile market, it will make you crazy!) Just remember the market adage "Buy low, sell high." It is rarely a good idea to sell just after a major market drop or correction. Use the tools we've mentioned—industry group rotation, support and resistance lines, expert market commentary—to gauge market conditions, and hang in there until it turns around.

# WEB SITES FOR KEEPING UP WITH THE MARKET

| | |
|---|---|
| ABC News | www.abcnews.com |
| American City Business Journals | www.amcity.com |
| American Stock Exchange | www.amex.com |

| | |
|---|---|
| Bloomberg | www.bloomberg.com |
| Briefing.com | www.briefing.com |
| Business Week | www.businessweek.com |
| CBS MarketWatch | cbs.marketwatch.com/news/<br>newsroom.htx |
| CNBC | www.cnbc.com |
| CNNfn | www.cnnfn.com |
| The Financial Center | www.tfc.com |
| Fination.com | www.fination.com |
| Forbes | www.forbes.com |
| Fortune.com | www.fortune.com |
| Fox News | www.foxnews.com |
| Hulbert Financial Digest | www.hulbertdigest.com |
| Individual Investor Online | www.iionline.com |
| INVESTools | www.investools.com |
| ISDEX | http://fastquote.com/groups/<br>isdex.html |
| The Internet Stock<br>Report | www.internetnews.com/stocks |
| Market Guide Investor | www.marketguide.com |
| Market Mavens Report | www.marketmavensreport.com |
| Money Talks | www.talks.com |
| The Motley Fool | www.fool.com |
| MSN Investor | www.investor.msn.com |
| MSNBC | www.msnbc.com |
| NASDAQ | www.nasdaq.com |
| National Association of<br>Securities Dealers | www.nasd.com |
| News.com | www.news.com |
| Newspage | www.newspage.com |
| New York Stock Exchange | www.nyse.com |
| The New York Times | www.nytimes.com |
| PersonalWealth.com | www.personalwealth.com |
| Quote.com | www.quote.com |

| | |
|---|---|
| Red Herring Online | www.redherring.com |
| Reuters Moneynet | www.moneynet.com |
| The Russell Indexes | www.russell.com |
| SmartMoney.com | www.smartmoney.com |
| Snap.com | www.snap.com |
| StockSite | www.stocksite.com |
| TheStreet.com | www.thestreet.com |
| StreetNet | www.streetnet.com |
| USA Today | www.usatoday.com |
| Wall Street City | www.wallstreetcity.com |
| The Wall Street Journal Interactive Edition | www.wsj.com |
| Yahoo! | www.yahoo.com |
| ZDNet | www.zdnet.com |

## Chapter 6

# The Online Brokers
## Trading on the Web

The Internet is sparking a genuine revolution in one corner of the investing world: the brokerage houses. With the beginning of Web-based trading in 1995, broker commissions started tumbling like rocks in an avalanche as investors discovered they could place their own buy and sell orders for a fraction of the cost of broker-assisted trades.

That price war among online brokers seems to have settled out to a range of about $5 to $30 a trade, and investors are signing up for online accounts in record numbers. In 1998 there were some 5.2 million online investors; that number is expected to grow to more than 22 million by the year 2002.

The rapid growth of online trading is grounded in several converging events. One, investors are gaining more confidence in Internet security and no longer view the Net as a big black hole that sucks up credit cards and digital dollars. Two, investors and other users are becoming more Internet-literate. This increase in literacy and confidence in Web security has boosted electronic commerce into the billion-dollar realm (even before the 1998 holiday shopping boom). Once you've bought a book from Amazon.com, it's only a small leap to placing your own trades. All it takes is confidence in online brokers to handle your trade on high-traffic days.

That test first came on October 27, 1997, a day on which the market melted down on the news of a market crash in Hong Kong. Web-based brokers in general got low marks. Some of the biggest names couldn't handle the high volume of traffic, and many investors were met with busy

## Is It Safe?

Safety is the number one concern of those who would send confidential information or digitized dollars over the Net. Is it safe? is the first question that comes to mind when we think about trading stocks online. The general consensus seems to be, yes, it is safe.

Nothing is foolproof, of course, but many measures have been taken by "those in charge" to enhance the safety and confidentiality of e-commerce. Web sites that deal in financial transactions or other confidential information use the industry standard protocol—*Secure Sockets Layer* (*SSL*)—to encode and decode the data transmitted between their Web site and the user's computer. The protocol uses a pair of asymmetric keys— a *public key* and a *private key*—developed by RSA Laboratories to encrypt and decrypt data. In short:

1. A Web site is issued a security certificate by an independent third party, usually Verisign, Inc. (www.verisign.com). The certificate is authenticated by the Web site's digital signature, which tells the inquiring computer that the Web site is who it says it is.

2. To communicate with a secure site (or a secure section of a site), you must have a secure browser, one that supports 40-bit or 128-bit encryption. The 128-bit encryption is more secure—a hacker would have to perform billions of calculations to crack the code, according to the software developers.

3. When you enter a secure site or a secure area on a site, your browser lets you know you're in a secure area by displaying a URL that begins with https:// rather than http://, and an unbroken key icon in the status line of your browser.

4. The encoded data then flows safely between you and the secure site.

You can read more about SSL and the whole issue of security at the Web site of one of "those in charge": RSA Laboratories (www.rsa.com).

**e-Commerce**   Electronic commerce is expected to reach $433 billion by 2001.

signals that caused them to miss important trades. But 10 months later, in August of 1998, the highest-volume trading day in history caused nary a glitch. The difference was primarily due to technological upgrades made by online brokers during the interim.

The upshot of all this is, Internet trading seems to have found its legs, and it is here to stay.

We are not suggesting that you have to trade online to take advantage of the Web's wealth of investing resources. But if you find your own investment ideas, research your own stocks, and manage your portfolio online, you would do yourself an injustice if you didn't at least consider online trading. This chapter will, hopefully, remove some of its mystery.

**Secure Browsers**   Secure browsers include Netscape Navigator 3.0 and 4.0, Microsoft Explorer 3.0 and 4.0, and America Online 3.0. The later versions use the 128-bit encryption.

## ANATOMY OF AN ONLINE BROKER

There were, at last count, some 80 online brokers. Some are brokerage arms of banks or mutual fund families, and many are niche players that cater to futures traders or day traders. About 30 or so are mainstream online brokers. The 9 that hold almost 90 percent of the market share in the online trading industry are listed on page 134.

In this chapter, we're going to examine one of the most highly rated of the mainstream discount brokers, DLJ*direct*, a company of Donaldson, Lufkin & Jenrette. DLJ*direct* has received the highest four-star rating from *Barron's* and is always among the top brokers in media surveys. Let's start with DLJ's home page at www.dljdirect.com (Figure 6.1).

DLJ*direct's* home page is a *newbie's* dream, with several clearly marked choices for visitors seeking information: two excellent demos, one for the portfolio and one for trades; inviting links, such as How Can I

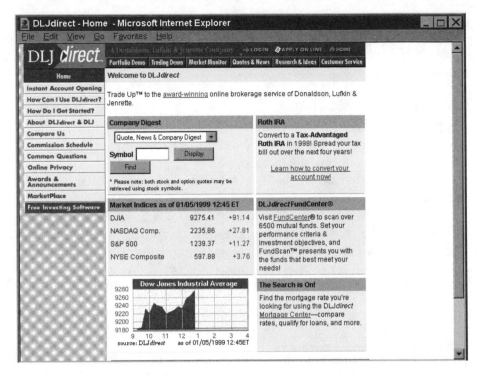

**FIGURE 6.1** DLJ*direct*'s home page isn't flashy, but it's clear, straightforward, and easy to navigate. (Reprinted with permission of DLJ*direct*, Inc. Copyright © 1998 DLJ*direct*, Inc. All rights reserved. Member SIPC and NASD. Trademarks of DLJ Long Term Investment Corporation.)

Use DLJ*direct*?, How Do I Get Started?, Compare Us (i.e., DLJ compared to other brokers); Common Questions, asked and answered; and a commission schedule that's just one mouse click away. (You'd be surprised how deeply commission schedules are sometimes buried.)

**Newbie** A new user of the Internet. A cyber-rookie, so to speak.

Let's start by exploring the demos.

**The Trading Demo** The nicest thing an online broker can do for a new investor is to provide a hands-on demo. Nothing will alleviate your fears about trading online like clicking your way through actual trading screens before you use them. DLJ*direct* gets an A+ in this category.

The trading demo takes you through the entire order entry process, and unlike other demos that just show you screens, DLJ lets you click through a sample order. It's the touchy-feely part of the demo that we think is so outstanding.

Let's click our way through the order entry screen for stock trades (Figure 6.2).

1. Enter the stock symbol and click Get Quote for a real-time quote. (If you don't know the symbol, enter the company name and click Lookup.) DLJ displays the company name and details on the pricing: bid/ask, last trade, change from the previous day's close, whether it was a *tick* up or tick down, and the exchange.

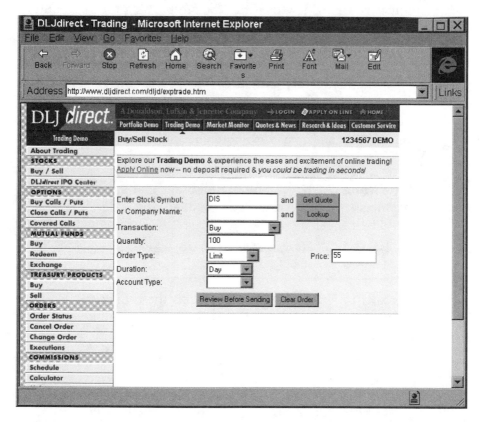

**FIGURE 6.2** The order entry screen at DLJ*direct* lets you enter market, limit, or stop orders. (Reprinted with permission of DLJ*direct*, Inc. Copyright © 1998 DLJ*direct*, Inc. All rights reserved. Member SIPC and NASD. Trademarks of DLJ Long Term Investment Corporation.)

2. Use the drop-down menu to select the type of transaction. Buy and Sell from Account are the most common. DLJ also allows for short sell trades.

3. Enter the number of shares.

4. Select the type of order. (DLJ allows *market orders*, *limit orders*, *stop orders*, *all or none (AON)*, and *fill or kill*. A few brokers allow *partial fill* and *stop-limit orders*.) Enter the desired price for limit and stop orders.

5. Select the duration of the order. DLJ allows *good till canceled (GTC)* and *day orders*.

6. Select the account type. DLJ's choices are cash account, *margin account*, or short account (the latter is for short sellers).

7. You're ready to send the order, but DLJ, like most Web brokers, forces you to review the order before pressing the Send button. Click the Review Before Sending button to double-check your order (Figure 6.3).

8. Now all you have to do is check the data, take a deep breath, and click the Send Order button. To change the order, click the Back button. To cancel it, click the Clear Order button.

9. What you get next is a confirmation screen that repeats the order information and gives you a reference number.

**All or None (AON)**   A buy or sell order that specifies that unless the entire order can be filled, the order should be canceled.

**Fill or Kill**   A buy order that instructs the broker to complete the trade by the end of the current trading day or cancel it.

**Partial Fill**   A limit order that is only partially filled because the total specified shares could not be bought or sold at the specified price.

**Stop-Limit Order**   A variation on the stop order; a stop-limit order will be executed only at the limit price, not higher or lower than the limit price. In contrast, a stop order will be executed at the stop price, or, should the stock gap up or down, at the higher- or lower-than-stop price.

 **Day Order**   An order to buy or sell a security that expires at the end of the day.

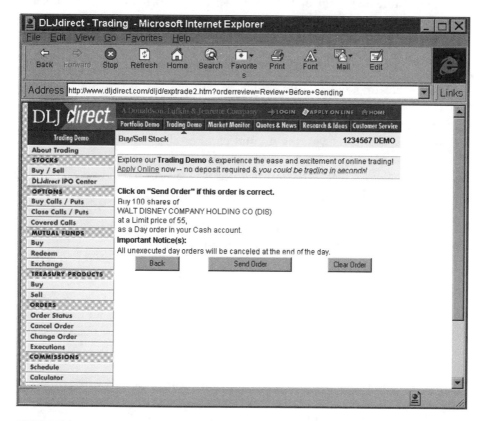

**FIGURE 6.3**   DLJ*direct*'s order review screen lets you confirm the order before sending it. (Reprinted with permission of DLJ*direct*, Inc. Copyright © 1998 DLJ*direct*, Inc. All rights reserved. Member SIPC and NASD. Trademarks of DLJ Long Term Investment Corporation.)

Your part is as easy as that. What happens next depends on whether the order is a market or limit order. A market order is zapped instantaneously to the computer system at the designated stock exchange and executed on a first-come, first-served basis. A limit order also goes directly to the exchange's computers but is put in a holding area until the stock price reaches your limit price; it is then executed on a first-come, first-served basis at that price.

There are exceptions. Each broker sets certain flags that generate rejection notices from the computer. For example, DLJ*direct* flags all stocks priced less than $1 to make sure that sufficient funds are in your account to cover the entire purchase price. In other words, penny stocks are not marginable. Recently, brokers have begun making certain highflying Internet stocks nonmarginable as well. Lack of sufficient funds in your account will generate a rejection of the order. Very large orders are also checked against the funds in your account to make sure the order is covered.

**The Portfolio Demo** DLJ's portfolio demo has the same interactivity as the trading demo. The one drawback is less-than-timely updates. DLJ*direct* portfolios are updated nightly, which means the trades you make during the day and the price changes in your stocks do not appear until the next day. Some portfolios, such as those of E*Trade and Web Street Securities, are updated whenever you log on and can be refreshed while you are online. The trend appears to be moving toward real-time updates. Four important portfolio screens are shown in Figures 6.4, 6.5, 6.6, and 6.7.

DLJ offers free downloadable software to enhance screens, increase speed, obtain real-time order status, and plot intraday and historical charts. You can also interface a DLJ portfolio with the offline Quicken or Microsoft Money software, as we discussed in Chapter 4.

## The Commission Schedule

Commissions are not the only measure by which to judge an online broker, but low commissions are a major attraction. You may need to draw deeply on your well of patience, however, when you start to compare online commissions.

Commission schedules can be very complicated, with different prices for market orders versus limit orders, different prices for large and small trades, and different definitions of large and small.

For example, DLJ*direct* charges a $20 commission for trades of 1000 shares or less. For larger trades, they add 2 cents a share. That means a trade of, say, 2500 shares would cost $50. And for stocks priced less than

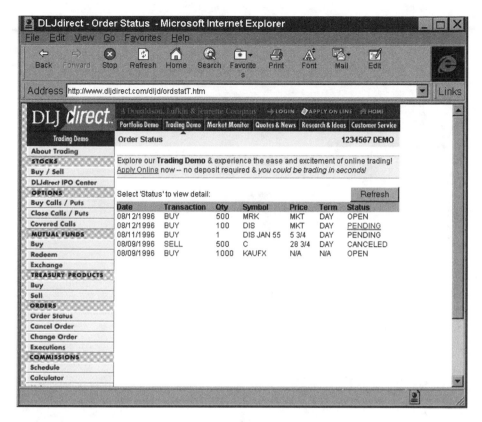

**FIGURE 6.4** The Order Status screen shows you the status of all outstanding orders. Pending orders can be revised or canceled. (Reprinted with permission of DLJ*direct*, Inc. Copyright © 1998 DLJ*direct*, Inc. All rights reserved. Member SIPC and NASD. Trademarks of DLJ Long Term Investment Corporation.)

$1—the so-called *penny stocks*—you may pay a surcharge up to 5 percent of the principal.

**Penny Stocks Surcharges** Penny stocks generally trade for less than $3/share, but brokers vary on where they draw the line for imposing a surcharge for trading such stocks. Some charge extra on stocks priced below $3; others on stocks below $2 or $1.

On the other hand, Web Street Securities (www.webstreetsecurities) charges $14.95 per trade for any *listed stock* of any size and for NASDAQ

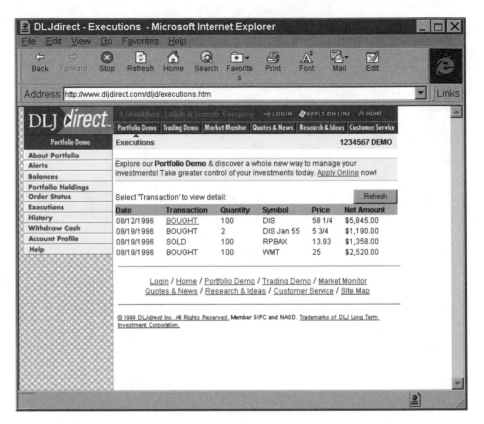

**FIGURE 6.5** The Executions screen displays the most recent trades. Click Bought or Sold under Transaction to view the details of the trade. (Reprinted with permission of DLJ*direct*, Inc. Copyright © 1998 DLJ*direct*, Inc. All rights reserved. Member SIPC and NASD. Trademarks of DLJ Long Term Investment Corporation.)

orders under 1000 shares. But NASDAQ trades of 1000 shares or more are free—if the stock is trading at $2 or more. Brokers that offer extremely low or free commissions usually depend on selling *order flow* to market makers who profit from the *spread* on NASDAQ stocks.

Then there's Fidelity's special price for active traders. Those who make 36 or more trades a year and maintain a minimum balance of $20,000 pay only $14.95 a trade. All others pay $25 a trade.

What's more, some brokers (none of the three just mentioned) add a service fee of $1.50 to $3 per trade, which effectively raises their commissions by that amount.

It may take a few hours of surfing and sizing up the players to discern all the nuances of online commissions. You can get a head start by studying CyberInvest.com's Broker Guides at www.cyberinvest.com and

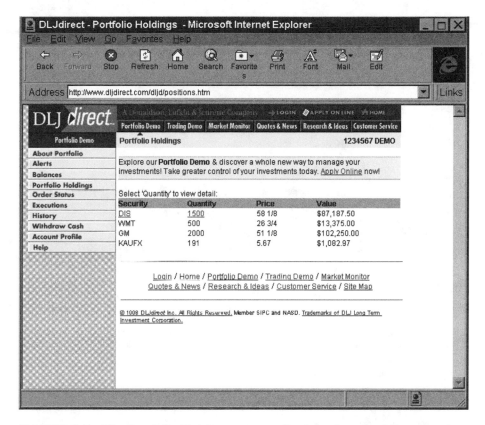

**FIGURE 6.6** The Portfolio Holdings screen displays the securities owned, along with the valuations. (Reprinted with permission of DLJ*direct*, Inc. Copyright © 1998 DLJ*direct*, Inc. All rights reserved. Member SIPC and NASD. Trademarks of DLJ Long Term Investment Corporation.)

then checking out the brokers that appear to be the best *for you*. The "Tips for Selecting an Online Broker" on pages 130 to 132 may be of some help in separating the wheat from the chaff.

**Security FAQ** Most brokers address the issue of security on their sites. Quick & Reilly (www.quickwaynet. com) has a good overview in its Help & Info section.

## Investing Tools

Another measure of an online broker's worth is the quantity and quality of its investing tools. These include all the tools we talked about in previous

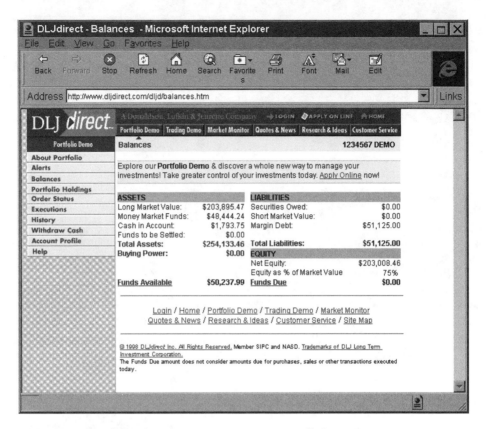

**FIGURE 6.7** The Balances screen summarizes all the activity in your account. (Reprinted with permission of DLJ*direct*, Inc. Copyright © 1998 DLJ*direct*, Inc. All rights reserved. Member SIPC and NASD. Trademarks of DLJ Long Term Investment Corporation.)

chapters, and they run the gamut from none to a well-stocked arsenal, and from free to pay-extra-for-everything.

In general, the higher the commission, the greater the array of investing tools. Deep discounter Brown & Co., with its flat commission of $5 for market orders, has zero tools and is proud of it. The upper-level discounters, like Charles Schwab and Accutrade (both at $29.95/trade) offer a wide array of resources, some free and some not. We don't have the space to catalog who has what, but we can give you some broad guidelines:

1. *Real-Time versus Delayed Quotes.* Real-time quotes should be available for making a trade. (The Web-wide trend is moving toward unlimited free real-time quotes.) Delayed quotes for portfolio updates are probably fine for everyone but day traders.

### Real-Time Quotes

The term "real-time quotes" on the Internet can be confusing. A Web site that advertises "free real-time quotes" offers one quote at a time, on demand, often with a limit of 50 quotes a day. This kind of real-time quote is a snapshot, so to speak, of the most recent trade. Another type of real-time quotes is by subscription (between $20 and $30 a month). For this you'll get real-time quotes on demand, with no limitation, or you can set up a portfolio to refresh the real-time quotes every X-number of minutes. A third type of real-time quotes is the continuous, live-feed quotes. This service, which costs a hundred dollars a month or more, provides a tick-by-tick updating of the quotes on your screen; each time a trade is made, your screen reflects that trade.

The question is: Does the average online investor need to subscribe to real-time quotes? Our answer is: not really. If you're placing a trade online, your online broker will supply free real-time quotes for that trade. And many brokers give bonus real-time quotes that go into a quote bank for later use. There are three exceptions that would, in our opinion, justify a subscription to real-time quotes: (1) very short-term trading where minute changes in the stock price are critical; (2) trading stocks with a very thin float, where an order might cause a large fluctuation in the stock price; and (3) intraday trading of any volatile stock which exhibits very rapid price fluctuations during a single day, such as the Internet stocks in late 1998/early 1999.

2. *Historical Charts.* These are important for research, but if your broker doesn't have them you can get them without charge at most investing supersites.

3. *Market Updates and Commentary.* Any broker worth its commissions should offer real-time or frequently updated market stats. But don't expect cutting-edge market commentary or news analysis unless the broker has partnered with a site like CBS MarketWatch or TheStreet.com. (Partnering is another trend in the making.)

4. *Investment Ideas.* The pickings are slim on most broker sites. Chances are, you'll have to mine the investing supersites for stock picks, screen, searches, and such.

5. *Research Tools.* Many brokers are partnering with research companies like EDGAR Online, First Call, Market Guide, S&P, Telescan, Zacks, and others to offer company profiles, earnings estimates, and other research tools. Some simply offer links to the partner's site (or a *cobranded page*) where you must subscribe to the service or purchase a report on a per-unit basis. A few brokers offer analyst research reports to qualified clients. For example, DLJ*direct* offers research reports from Donaldson, Lufkin & Jenrette free of charge to discount customers with six-digit accounts (with a free 30-day trial to all new accounts). Fidelity offers pay-per-view or subscriptions to Salomon Smith Barney research.

6. *Extras.* Online brokers offer many different freebies to attract your business: credit or debit cards, free check writing, free real-time quotes, personalized pages. Some get even more creative with frequent flier miles (Bull & Bear Securities) and free e-mail addresses (E*Trade). These won't make up for slow-loading pages or poor navigation, but hey! All other things being equal, why not go for the extras?

**Cobranded Page**   A page at a Web site that is cosponsored by another Web site.

Keep in mind, your broker doesn't have to meet all your investing needs. The entire World Wide Web is at your disposal, and it offers immediate, hassle-free access to all the investing tools mentioned in this book. Find a broker site you like with commissions that match your kind of trading; then fulfill the rest of your investing needs at one or two investing supersites. You, not the brokers, are in the catbird seat.

## And Consider This . . .

It is difficult to enjoy low commissions or reams of free research if a site is so slow or so difficult to navigate that you want to slam your fist through the monitor. Spend enough time on the site *before you open an account* to be sure it is a place you want to call your investing home.

Keep in mind, however, that slow-loading pages may not be the fault of the site. The age of your *browser*, your *Internet service provider (ISP)*, the speed of your modem, and the time of day are all involved. (Rush hours also occur in cyberspace.) But if Broker A appears before the word "slow" crosses your mind and Broker B materializes like a developing Polaroid, you can pretty much assume the slowness is inherent in the site. (Be sure you test them in the same five-minute period and that the fast-loading pages aren't stored in your *cache*.)

**Internet Service Provider (ISP)**   A company that provides software and communications links to the Internet. Two of the larger ISPs are Netcom and AT&T, but there are hundreds of smaller ISPs.

**Reasons for Slowness**   Heavy use of graphics can slow down a site, as can Java script that is used in some portfolios and scrolling tickers. Also, a slow-loading banner ad can stop a site cold until the banner is fully loaded.

The responsibility for site navigation—moving smoothly and logically from page to page—lies solely with the broker site. You can get some insight into these matters by consulting various broker ratings.

## RATING THE ONLINE BROKERS

Rating online brokers is a favorite pastime of the media and a few specialty Web sites. The ratings can be helpful in spotlighting the features that are most important to you. Keep in mind, however, that many of the ratings are subjective, and most brokers can claim a high rating in at least one category. Look for brokers that receive high ratings in more than one survey. Then check out the highest three or four for yourself. Here are some places to start:

### Tips for Selecting an Online Broker

Single-digit commissions may look attractive, but a bargain is a bargain only if it fits your needs as well as your wallet. Here are 13 points to consider when selecting an online broker.

1. ***Size matters.*** If your average trade is 100 or 500 shares, check the broker's commission schedule for trades of those sizes. Sometimes the highly touted low rates (or commissionless trades) apply only to trades of 1000 or 5000 shares. Or they may apply only to accounts of a certain size, or only for NASDAQ stocks, only for market orders, or only for stocks trading above a certain price. You get the picture.

2. ***Check out the fees.*** Brokers charge for many things besides commissions. Some tack a postage and handling fee or transaction fee onto all trades. Most charge for wire transfers and issuing a stock certificate in your name, but there are more esoteric fees as well. If a fee schedule is not posted online, ask for one before you sign up.

3. ***It depends on what they mean by zero.*** Some brokers boast that they require zero funds to open an account. All that means is you can fill out the forms and open the account. But, you can't make a trade without sufficient funds in your account unless you have a credit line. IRA accounts usually require lower minimums and options accounts higher minimums than regular accounts.

4. ***If you want kiwis, be sure to plant a kiwi tree.*** And if you regularly trade mutual funds, options, bonds, or IPOs, make sure you select a broker that supports those kinds of securities. Some require broker assistance, which may mean a higher commission.

5. *Talk the talk.* Make sure you know a market order from a limit order, a GTC from a day order. (Many brokers have glossaries on their sites.) If you plan to use stop orders (see Chapter 4), be sure to choose a broker that accepts them.

6. *Point, click, trade?* Find out what happens after you click the Submit Order key. Some firms require a human broker to review trades, which will slow down the process. In a fast-paced market, a delay in executing a trade can cost you money.

7. *Checks, sweeps, and interest rates.* Ask potential brokers these questions: What is the interest rate paid on the idle funds in your account? Are idle funds swept automatically into an interest-bearing account each day? Can you write checks on the account? Without charge?

8. *Look for rewards.* If you make several trades a month, consider a broker that rewards active traders. Some reduce commissions; others give incentives like Frequent Flier miles. Keep in mind that each broker defines "active" in its own terms.

9. *Stretch your buying power.* A margin account lets you borrow against the equity in the account. Interest is charged on the borrowed funds, so be sure to factor in the margin rate when you're considering a broker's commission level.

10. *Tools of the trade.* Consider the range and the cost of investing tools offered by the broker. You may get a better deal by going with the lowest commission and doing your research elsewhere on the Web.

11. *Check the security.* Read the site's FAQ (Frequently Asked Questions) on security, and look

(*continued*)

for the security flags when you trade (see "Is It Safe?" on page 116). Also, be sure the broker is a member of the *National Association of Securities Dealers (NASD)* and the *Securities Investor Protection Corporation (SIPC)*.

12. ***Check customer support.*** In a crunch it all comes down to customer support. Is an 800 customer service number listed prominently on the site? Is there a live human on the other end of the line to answer your urgent questions, or at least an option on the voice menu to reach one? How responsive is the broker to an e-mail? Test it before you sign up.

13. ***Open a backup account.*** What are the broker's emergency backup measures when the Internet is overloaded or down? Touch-Tone telephone? Personal broker? Consider opening a second account at a different broker for backup.

✔ *SmartMoney.com*'s Broker Ratings (www.smartmoney.com—Figure 6.8), updated several times a year.

✔ *Barron's Online*'s annual Broker Ratings (www.barrons.com), published annually in March.

✔ *Kiplinger.com*'s Broker Ratings (www.kiplinger.com), published in October 1998.

✔ *The Motley Fool*'s Brokerage Center (www.fool.com).

✔ *The Wall Street Journal Interactive Edition*'s special report on online trading (www.wsj.com), published in September 1998.

✔ *Money.com*'s "Guide to Online Investing" (www.money.com), published in the summer of 1998.

✔ *Gomez Advisors'* Internet Broker Scorecard (www.gomezwire.com), published quarterly.

✔ *Keynote Systems'* Online Brokerage Index (www.keynote.com) rates the performance and reliability of 20 online brokers weekly.

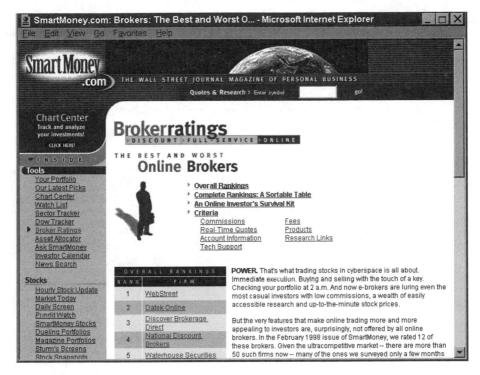

**FIGURE 6.8** Online broker ratings from SmartMoney.com. (Reprinted with permission of SmartMoney.com. © 1996–1999 SmartMoney. SmartMoney is a joint publishing venture of Dow Jones & Company, Inc. and The Hearst Corporation.)

## OPENING AN ACCOUNT

You've read all the articles on the best online brokers. You've compared commissions and investing tools till you're cross-eyed and muddle-headed. Now it's time to make a commitment. You're ready to open your first online account. Here are the steps.

1. *Decide on the amount of your initial investment.* Online brokers vary widely in their requirements for the initial investment, ranging from zero (12 out of 30 brokers) to $15,000 (Brown & Co.). The average is about $2000 for a non-IRA account, less for IRAs (individual retirement accounts). (With zero initial investment, don't expect to trade stocks until sufficient funds to cover the trade are in your account.) You can, of course, deposit securities rather than cash to meet the minimum investment.

## Top Brokers by Market Share

Nine brokers dominated the online trading industry at the end of the fourth quarter 1998, together commanding 89 percent of the market. All appear among the top-rated brokers in one or more of the broker surveys mentioned on page 132. We list them here for your comparison.

| Broker | Market Share | Minimum to Open Account | Minimum Commission for Web-Based Trades of More Than 1000 shares |
|---|---|---|---|
| Charles Schwab & Co. www.schwab.com | 27.4% | $5000 | $29.95 |
| Waterhouse Securities www.waterhouse.com | 12.4 | 2000 | 12.00 |
| E*Trade www.etrade.com | 11.8 | 1000 | 14.95 |
| Datek Online www.datek.com | 10.0 | 2000 | 9.99 |
| Fidelity Investments www.fidelity.com | 9.4 | 5000 | 14.95 (active traders) |
| Ameritrade www.ameritrade.com | 7.6 | 2000 | 8.00 |
| DLJdirect www.dljdirect.com | 3.7 | 0 | 20.00 |
| Quick & Reilly www.quickwaynet.com | 3.4 | 0 | 14.95 |
| Discover Brokerage Direct www.discoverbrokerage.com | 3.3 | 2000 | 14.95 |

(Market share data from a report by Credit Suisse First Boston Corporation. Quoted with permission.)

2. *Decide on the type of account.* Online brokers offer the same range of accounts as offline brokers: individual accounts, corporate accounts, custodial accounts, joint accounts, cash accounts, margin accounts, option accounts, IRAs, 401(k)s, and others. Account types should be explained at the broker site. If not, call or ask for help by e-mail.

3. *Complete the application.* More and more sites are offering online applications, although some require you to request or download forms and mail in the completed and signed application. Online applications are quick and easy. Just be sure your application is in a secure part of the site. (See "Is It Safe?" on page 116.) To view an example of an online application, go to DLJ*direct* or E*Trade.

4. *Deposit or transfer securities or funds.* Whether you complete an online application or send it by regular mail, you must deposit funds or securities the old-fashioned way: by check or by wire. Processing the initial check can take five days or longer, and transferring securities from another broker requires a special form and can take several weeks to process. So don't expect to make a trade the day, or even the week, you open the account. No doubt in the future all this will be done electronically.

5. *Wait for notification of your user ID number and password.* You can't make that first trade until funds are received and your user ID number and password have been approved and assigned to your account. You'll be notified by e-mail or regular mail when your account is activated.

While you're waiting for account approval, try your hand at one of the simulated trading games to hone your skills and increase your confidence.

## THE TRADING GAMES

Simulated stock market games are an excellent way to develop skills and gain confidence in placing trades without risking your life savings. Registration is required, but the games are free. Here are two of the best: CNN's Final Bell and The Game at E*Trade.

### *CNNfn's Final Bell*

The Final Bell stock simulation game (Figure 6.9) is a joint venture of CNN and Sandbox Entertainment (www.finalbell.com). It offers one of

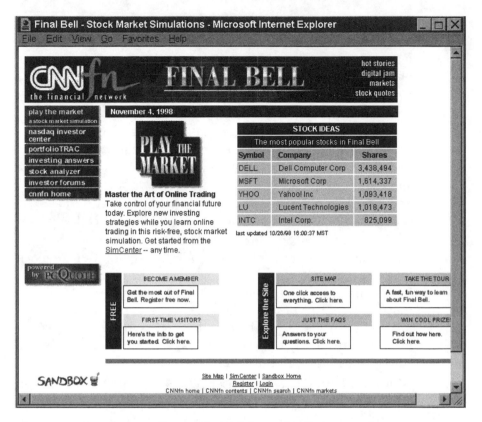

**FIGURE 6.9** The home page of CNNfn's Final Bell. (Copyright © 1998 Time Inc. New Media. All rights reserved. Reproduction in whole or in part without permission is prohibited. Pathfinder is a registered trademark of Time Inc. New Media.)

the most realistic trading environments of any of the games, allowing the same types of orders as most online brokers. But unlike a broker order screen, Final Bell has great help screens. The Buying and Selling Examples on the Order Entry screen make you feel as if a market guru is whispering helpful hints in your ear as you trade. Other useful tools include checklists, strategy tools, a glossary, and several educational articles. Each game lasts several weeks, and players compete for prizes that include PCs, laptops, Palm Pilots, and T-shirts.

### The E*Trade Game

At E*Trade (www.etrade.com) you can play a stock game or a stock and options game. Each starts you off with $100,000 of play money, and you can compete for $1000 in real money. Winners are chosen monthly, based on their portfolio value at the end of the month.

Figure 6.10 shows the main game page, which can be customized with your favorite stocks and Web site. The navigation bar on the left links to the trading screens and the game account screens that track your holdings.

## And Consider These . . .

You may also want to check out these games:

✔ *The Virtual Stock Exchange.* (www.virtualstockexchange.com) Trade stocks and mutual funds on realistic trading screens.

✔ *MarketPlayer.com.* (www.marketplayer.com) You can buy, sell, or sell short in this "Hedgehog Competition," using a preselected database of 3600 stocks (over $5 in price and over $75 in market cap). There's a large statistical database for these stocks and a

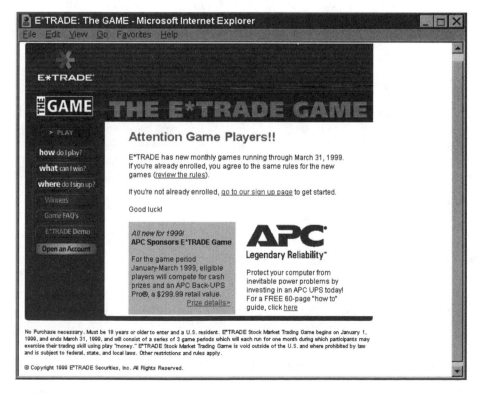

**FIGURE 6.10** The main menu of E*Trade's stock market game. (Reprinted with permission of E*Trade.)

screening program to help you find your winners. Trading screens, however, are simplistic.

✔ *Edustock.* (http://library.advanced.org/3088) Do simulated trading of any stock on the NYSE, NASDAQ, or AMEX.

✔ *Stock-Trak.* (www.stocktrak.com) Originally a college teaching tool, Stock-Trak offers a WWW simulation for individual investors. You can trade domestic or international stocks, options, futures, bonds, and mutual funds. A new competition starts on the first Monday of each month and lasts for a 12-week period. The cost is $19.95 per competition.

✔ *VCExchange.com.* (www.vcexchange.com) Trade IPOs, although it is more of an IPO-picking contest than simulated trading.

✔ *Global Strategist.* (www.global-strategist.com) This one is expensive: $40 a month to trade global stocks and bonds as a group in various countries (not actual stocks or bonds).

✔ *MainXchange.* (www.mainxchange.com) This is a stock market simulation game aimed at teenagers, with prizes from sponsors like Continental Airlines, Tommy Hilfiger, and Planet Hollywood.

✔ *Hollywood Stock Exchange.* (www.hsx.com) For movie buffs only, trade virtual stocks in real movies. A tutorial explains it all.

Stock market simulations are an excellent way to practice your trading skills without any risk. Use them as a learning tool until you're ready for the real thing.

## SUMMARY

Online trading can be empowering, but we caution you against feeling too powerful. Studies have shown that investors who trade online make five times as many trades as investors who use a personal broker. It could be that those frequent traders carefully screen and research their stocks and time their trades to minimize risk and maximize reward. Or it could be that the ease of it all has transformed their computers into the equivalent of a slot machine. We urge you to plant yourself firmly in the first group and treat online trading with the care and caution it deserves.

We've come to the end of the online investing process as it applies to stocks. Now we'll move on to mutual funds and other investments that have been made more accessible by the Internet.

## WEB SITES FOR TRADING ON THE WEB

| | |
|---|---|
| American Express Financial Direct | www.americanexpress.com/direct |
| Ameritrade | www.ameritrade.com |
| Barron's Online | www.barrons.com |
| Bull & Bear Securities | www.bullbear.com |
| CNNfn's Final Bell | www.finalbell.com |
| CyberInvest.com | www.cyberinvest.com |
| Datek | www.datek.com |
| Discover Brokerage Direct | www.discoverbrokerage.com |
| DLJ*direct* | www.dljdirect.com |
| Edustock | http://library.advanced.org/3088 |
| E*Trade | www.etrade.com |
| Fidelity Investments | www.fidelity.com |
| Global Strategist | www.global-strategist.com |
| Gomez Advisors | www.gomezwire.com |
| Hollywood Stock Exchange | www.hsx.com |
| Keynote Systems | www.keynote.com |
| Kiplinger.com | www.kiplinger.com |
| MainXchange | www.mainxchange.com |
| MarketPlayer.com | www.marketplayer.com |
| Money.com | www.money.com |
| The Motley Fool | www.fool.com |
| Quick & Reilly | www.quick-reilly.com |
| RSA Laboratories | www.rsa.com |
| Charles Schwab & Co. | www.schwab.com |
| SmartMoney.com | www.smartmoney.com |
| Stock-Trak | www.stocktrak.com |
| VCExchange.com | www.vcexchange.com |

| | |
|---|---|
| Verisign, Inc. | www.verisign.com |
| Virtual Stock Exchange | www.virtualstockexchange.com |
| The Wall Street Journal Interactive Edition | www.wsj.com |
| Waterhouse Securities | www.waterhouse.com |
| Web Street Securities | www.webstreetsecurities.com |

# Mutual Fund Madness
## Where the Funds Are

B.T.I.—before the Internet—if you wanted to invest in a mutual fund, you probably stuck to household names, like Fidelity or Vanguard, or asked your stockbroker or banker for a recommendation. If you wanted more hands-on involvement, you went to the library and looked up the Morningstar ratings and read a few reports on the highest-rated funds. If you were really ambitious you might have subscribed to a mutual fund newsletter. By the time the 1980s rolled around, you may have graduated to computerized screening. It wasn't that big a deal then since there weren't that many funds to choose from.

Well, hang on to your mouse pad; this isn't your father's mutual fund world anymore.

Mutual funds have exploded in a frenzy of growth over the past few years, from 564 funds in 1980 with assets of $135 billion to more than 9000 in 1998 with assets exceeding $5 trillion. That's nearly as many funds as stocks, and, like stocks, their performance varies greatly. Finding the best mutual fund in this expanding universe presents a challenge indeed.

Fortunately, the World Wide Web happened along, and dozens of Web sites have materialized to guide you through the new mutual fund cyberworld. In addition, the majority of *mutual fund families* have established their own Web sites, where they compete for your attention not only with their funds but also with a wide array of planning tools and educational materials.

In this chapter, we will review briefly the process of building and managing a mutual fund portfolio; then we'll show you the best Web sites for helping you do it online.

## BUILDING A MUTUAL FUND PORTFOLIO

Building a mutual fund portfolio is similar in many ways to building a stock portfolio. First, you have to consider your investment goals, your tolerance for risk, and your time horizon. Then you have to find the best funds to match these requirements, evaluate them, buy them, and monitor them. If you are new to mutual fund investing, we recommend that you read a good book or article on the basics. The American Association of Individual Investors (AAII) has an excellent series of articles on mutual fund investing at www.aaii.com (for members). There is also a wealth of free educational material at fund family sites, which are discussed later in this chapter.

 **Long-Term Investors**   Mutual fund investors are, generally speaking, long-term investors.

 **AAII Membership**   Membership in the American Association of Individual Investors costs $49/year. For more information, visit the AAII site at www.aaii.com.

To get you started, however, and to give you an idea of what to expect from the sites you'll learn about in this chapter, we have distilled the mutual fund investing process to 10 essential steps. Many of these steps apply to other kinds of investing as well.

### Step 1: Know Thyself

It is important to know what you expect out of a mutual fund portfolio. What are your investment goals? Are you aggressive? Or are you a patient accumulator? How much risk can you stomach? Do you want to maximize your returns or minimize your risk? Do large, established fund families with long track records attract you? Or are you comfortable with smaller funds with good but short-term performance?

Fund family Web sites offer many free tools to help you find answers to these questions. The tools are often simple questionnaires, but they can be helpful in illuminating your capacity for risk. Morningstar.Net, by the way, has an excellent six-part article on risk, called "Risky Business." You'll find it under Funds 101 in Morningstar's Learn section (www. morningstar.net).

## Step 2: Determine the Portfolio Mix

A mutual fund, by definition, is diversified, since it is a collection of stocks or bonds. But you don't have to put all your money into one fund. With Internet tools, you will find it easy to diversify among several funds. According to the AAII, a good mix in a small portfolio would be four to nine funds: several domestic stock funds (divided among large cap, small cap, and various sectors), one or two domestic bond funds, an international stock fund, and an international bond fund.

## Step 3: Find a Fund

With more than 9000 funds to choose from, finding the right fund can be as much of a challenge these days as finding the right stock. To help you with this step, the Internet offers such tools as preset screens, customized searches, lists of top performers, recommendations from mutual fund experts, and funds in the news. The searches and screens are of particular importance. One search tool helps you find the funds that perform well in down markets or up markets. It also lets you search for funds by type (balanced, growth, income and growth, and so on), or by sector or industry. Funds can be compared within a category or by size and types of fees. Just as with stocks, you might want to try all these resources to create a list of prospects.

## Step 4: Do Your Homework

Once you have a list of prospects, you need to do your homework to decide which ones to buy. How? First, look at a *profile* of the fund. Profiles summarize pertinent information from the *prospectus*, such as *investment objective*, size, risk level, top 5 to 10 holdings, and performance. Once you've narrowed the list to the probables, check out the fees and sales charges. Prospectuses can be found at fund family Web sites or research sites described later in this chapter.

### Step 5: Consider the Independent Ratings

Several independent services rate mutual funds on various performance criteria. Morningstar rates funds from 1 to 5 based on mathematical calculations of past performance. Value Line ranks them on risk and reward. Lipper Analytical Services gives funds a Performance Quintile Rating for up markets, down markets, and the current market. Forbes gives letter grades (A through D) to domestic and foreign stock funds. SmartMoney also bestows letter grades on selected funds. You can read more about ratings in the site descriptions to follow.

### Step 6: Learn the Composition of the Fund

We feel like we're buying a pig in a poke if we don't know the companies owned by the mutual fund. In most cases, the top 5 or 10 holdings are listed on the fund profile. Some funds list their holdings in their annual or semiannual report, which is usually available at the fund's Web site. Keep in mind that it will be only a snapshot at a particular point in time.

Another way to learn the holdings is to use the X-Rays feature at Morningstar.Net (www.morningstar.net). Click Monitor, then Track Your Portfolio. And, if you're morally or philosophically opposed to owning tobacco stock, go to the Calvert Group (www.calvertgroup.com), where you can check the tobacco holdings (or the top 10 holdings) of any mutual fund.

### Step 7: Understand the Fees

*Load, no-load, front-end load, back-end load, 12b-1 fee, redemption fee, exchange fee, management fee, administrative fee.* Mutual funds fees are nothing if not confusing, but you need to understand them and factor them into the cost of the fund. Value Line (www.valueline.com) has an excellent article on fees and expenses in its Learn section.

**12b-1 Fee**   A fee deducted from a mutual fund's earnings to cover the fund's sales and marketing expenses.

**Exchange Fee** Fee charged by a mutual fund family for exchanging shares of one fund for shares of another. Also, fee charged by a stock exchange for dissemination of stock quotes.

**Open-End versus Closed-End Funds**

An open-end fund is an investment company that pools the money from shareholders and invests in a variety of securities. Shares in the fund are bought and sold on demand, based on the fund's closing net asset value (NAV) on the day of the trade. The fund families mentioned in this book (and most fund families) have open-end funds. A closed-end fund has a fixed number of shares. It is listed on a major stock exchange or NASDAQ and trades just like a stock, with the price of its shares determined by the market. Forbes (www.forbes.com) has a listing of closed-end mutual funds.

## Step 8: Purchase the Fund

The cheapest way to buy a mutual fund is through the mutual fund family. Most families cover a broad spectrum of investing strategies— from aggressive to conservative, from domestic to global—so you can diversify and switch funds with changing market conditions without ever leaving the family. Many funds allow you to purchase, exchange, and redeem funds online. Others offer an 800 number for telephone transactions.

You can also buy funds through most online brokers, from financial planners, and from "fund supermarkets," such as Schwab or Fidelity. Schwab's OneSource (Figure 7.1) or Fidelity's FundsNetwork offer funds from many different fund companies. This gives you a wider selection of funds without the inconvenience of dealing with several families.

Many fund families, by the way, have automatic investment plans that let you invest small sums of money at regular intervals, rather than large lump sums. This is called dollar-cost averaging. It reduces the effect

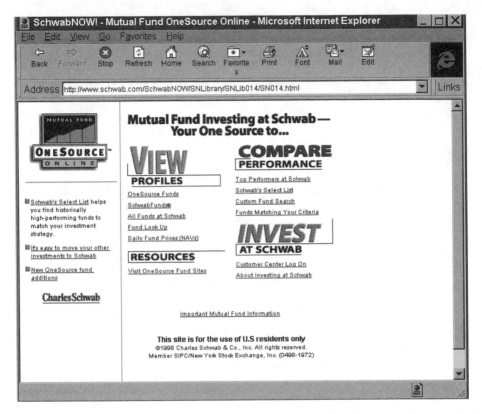

**FIGURE 7.1** Charles Schwab offers dozens of fund families and thousands of funds in its OneSource. (Reprinted with permission of Charles Schwab & Co., Inc.)

**Closing NAV** Mutual funds are purchased or sold once a day, based on the closing net asset value (NAV) of the fund. In other words, if you enter a sell order for a fund today, the sell price will be the closing NAV at the end of the day.

of market fluctuations by increasing the number of shares purchased at lower prices and decreasing the number purchased at higher prices. You can sign up for the automatic investment plan online at most fund families.

## Step 9: Monitor the Fund

Mutual fund investors are, generally speaking, in for the long haul. Holding a fund for five to ten years is not uncommon. Nevertheless, you'll want to monitor your funds at least quarterly. Here are some areas to consider.

✔ *Portfolio Changes.* Look at the changes in the portfolio mix. You're paying the manager for his or her expertise, so it is unlikely you would question the selections. But you should know what you own.

✔ *Changes in Fees.* Any new fees should be announced in the quarterly or annual report. Be sure you understand the purpose of each.

✔ *Change in Fund Managers.* If the fund has been performing well, a change in managers could signal a change in investing style, which could result in a deterioration of return. On the other hand, if the fund has been doing poorly, a change could herald a new beginning. Either way, you'll have to base your decision on the new manager's prior performance. Several Web sites mentioned in this chapter feature profiles of or interviews with fund managers. You might want to see if your fund manager is among them. Be aware that a manager may be associated with many funds and not be actively involved with each one.

✔ *Performance.* Compare your fund's annual performance against appropriate indexes or fund categories. The Mutual Fund Investor's Center has a list of comparative indexes for this purpose (Figure 7.2). It isn't prudent to judge a fund on a single quarter's performance, but deteriorating performance over several quarters could be a good reason to switch funds.

## Step 10: Sell or Exchange a Fund

When a fund fails one of the critical benchmarks—or whenever your goals change for any reason—you may want to redeem or exchange your shares. For example, you may want to switch to a better-performing sector or move from a large-cap fund to a small-cap fund. Fund families usually let you exchange one fund for another within the same family without incurring any additional fees.

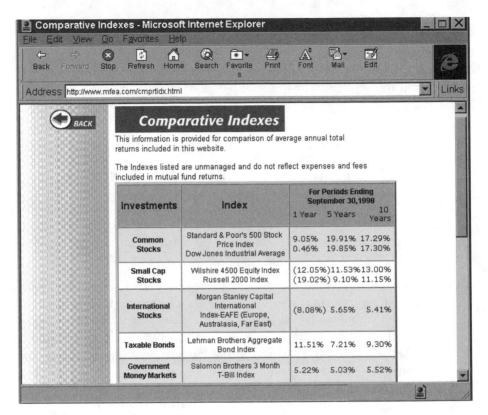

**FIGURE 7.2** These index returns offer a good benchmark for comparing the performance of mutual funds or your own portfolio. Scroll down to see a chart that shows average returns by fund category. (Reprinted with permission of Mutual Fund Education Alliance.)

In the remainder of this chapter, we'll look at Web sites that offer tools, resources, and educational material for the mutual fund investor. We've arbitrarily broken them down into three categories: the dedicated mutual fund sites, general investing sites with mutual fund centers, and mutual fund families.

## DEDICATED MUTUAL FUND SITES

A handful of sites focus primarily or exclusively on mutual funds, and you may wish to bookmark them for easy reference. Three are devoted exclusively to mutual funds—the Mutual Fund Investor's Center, Mutual Funds Interactive, and Mutual Funds Online—and two are closely

associated with mutual funds, even though they cover stocks as well—
Morningstar.net and Value Line. Let's look at tools and resources offered
by each.

## Mutual Fund Investor's Center

This is the Web site of the Mutual Fund Education Alliance
(www.mfea.com—Figure 7.3), and as you might guess it is loaded with
educational material. Its "Basics of Mutual Fund Investing," aimed at the
novice investor, is quite thorough with a good glossary. The Bookstore is a
handy one-stop shopping mall for free educational brochures from dozens
of funds and fund families. Topics include asset planning, international
investing, IRA planning, distributions, taxes, and investing for children,
college, and retirement.

The Center's search engine is good for finding funds with certain investment objectives. You can search by fund family or by category, and, if

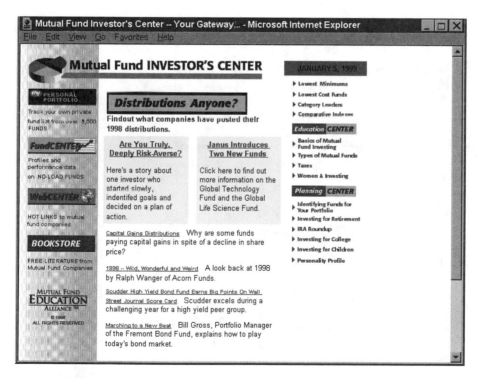

**FIGURE 7.3** The home page of the Mutual Fund Investor's Center.
(Reprinted with permission of Mutual Fund Education Alliance.)

you wish, specify investment minimums and various fees. You cannot, however, specify performance criteria, which makes narrowing funds to a workable list a bit difficult. For example, we searched for aggressive growth funds in all families and got back a list of 89 funds. Click on the name of a fund and you'll get a nicely formatted profile of the fund with a link to the fund's Web site.

### Brill's Mutual Funds Interactive

Brill's Mutual Funds Interactive (www.fundsinteractive.com—Figure 7.4) has an outstanding collection of columns and articles from mutual fund experts ("Tips on Finding Funds That May Do Better Than Most," "Funds for Tax-Averse Investors," "Uses and Abuses of Mutual Funds," to name three). You'll find them under Expert's Corner, Columns, and Musings. Rounding out this virtual minicourse on investing are live audio interviews (MFI Uncut), basic investing articles (Funds 101), and a glossary.

**FIGURE 7.4** The home page of Brill's Mutual Funds Interactive. (Reprinted with permission of Brill's Mutual Funds Interactive.)

Profiles of some 50 mutual fund managers give you an inside peek at their management strategies.

 **RealAudio Plug-In** RealAudio plug-in is downloadable software that enables your computer to play audio interviews. Click the RealAudio link at the Mutual Funds Interactive site or go directly to RealAudio at www.realaudio.com.

Brill's Mutual Funds Interactive has partnered with Value Line to offer fund snapshots and a fund screen, both free. (But you have to enter your e-mail address each time you use this section to acknowledge that you accept their terms and conditions.) The profiles include historical fund returns up to five years; Value Line fund ratings, which are based on risk and reward; the name of the fund manager, along with his or her rating and tenure; fund contact information; and maximum load percentage. The fund's Web site is not provided, but Brill's has links in a separate section to 80-some funds and fund families. (It would be nice to have a link to that section on the profile page.) The fund screen searches the Value Line database using a rather simplistic screen that allows you to specify ranges for the total return, Value Line rank, and maximum front-end load.

Another partner is BigCharts, which provides interactive charting for comparing a fund's performance to another fund or index. Finally, Brill's hosts several discussion groups where you can trade wit and wisdom with other fund investors.

## Mutual Funds Online

Much at Mutual Funds Online (www.mfmag.com) is free and most of it is excellent. The best free feature is a searchable archive that contains every *Mutual Funds* magazine since 1994 with hundreds of excellent educational articles on funds. You can locate articles by keyword search or by viewing the table of contents and then jumping to the articles of interest.

Other free tools include calculators, a glossary, and a listing of fund family Web sites and telephones. There's also a free message board and moderated chat sessions with fund experts.

There's more, but there are also premium features (at $9.95/

month): NAV quotes, fund profiles, performance rankings, special on-line articles, screening on more than 9000 funds, and a personalized page.

## Morningstar.Net

Morningstar.Net (www.morningstar.net) provides research on over 17,000 stocks and open- and closed-end mutual funds. There's a lot to like at this site, especially the excellent, original editorial content, but our favorite feature is the Quicktake Reports. The coolest thing about the report is its easy-to-use tabulated format (Figure 7.5): Click a tab to see the different information offered in that category. Some features of the Quick-take are free; some aren't. (Premium services are flagged with a + sign.) For example, the Morningstar rating and the NAV chart are free, but the

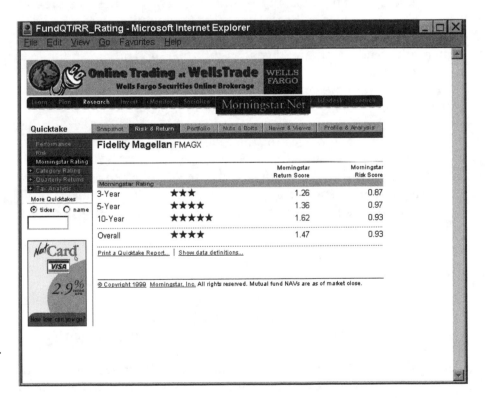

**FIGURE 7.5** The Risk & Return tab on this Quicktake Report shows the Morningstar rating for Fidelity Magellan on January 5, 1999. (Reprinted with permission of Morningstar, Inc.)

Morningstar analysis and Dow Jones news are part of the $9.95 monthly premium.

 **Morningstar Ratings** The Morningstar rating of one to five stars (five is high) is based on a mathematical measure of risk-adjusted return. Morningstar ratings have been criticized for being too weighted toward the long-term past performance of a fund and not sensitive enough to recent performance.

Many features are free: featured funds, dozens of articles both current and archived, and regular columns on funds and the fund industry. As for screening tools, the Fund Selector offers free basic screens on specific fund categories, but advanced screens with variable criteria are part of the site subscription.

## SUPERSITE FUND CENTERS

Many investing supersites mentioned in previous chapters also have outstanding mutual fund resources. Here are the best ones.

### CBS MarketWatch

There are a lot of good reasons to visit CBS MarketWatch's Mutual Fund Center (cbs.marketwatch.com/news/newsroom.htx—Figure 7.6)—fund profiles, fund news updated hourly, a plethora of columns and feature articles, interviews with top mutual fund managers, a fund alert feature that updates breaking news on mutual funds throughout the day, and the SuperStar Index of the top 100 best mutual funds for the buy-and-hold investor. But what we like best are the editorials by Dr. Paul B. Farrell, which are published online in what he calls "SuperStar Funds—the e-Book." It currently comprises some 20 chapters and is updated daily.

Possibly because of Dr. Farrell's A to Z coverage of mutual funds, the CBS MarketWatch Fund University is simply a brief collection of links to educational sites. But don't miss the interactive mutual fund IQ test that will show you exactly how much you know (or don't know) about mutual funds.

**FIGURE 7.6** The Mutual Fund Center at CBS MarketWatch. (Reprinted with permission of CBS MarketWatch.)

### PersonalWealth.com

The mutual funds section at PersonalWealth.com (www.personalwealth. com) is noteworthy for its educational articles. Some sample titles:

✔ "How to Survive a Market Correction."

✔ "Investing with Style."

✔ "Finding Income When Interest Rates Tumble."

Check out the archives under Fund Insight; Hot Fund Strategies; What's Hot, What's Not; and Fundamentals. Some are free, but the majority are part of the monthly $9.95 site subscription.

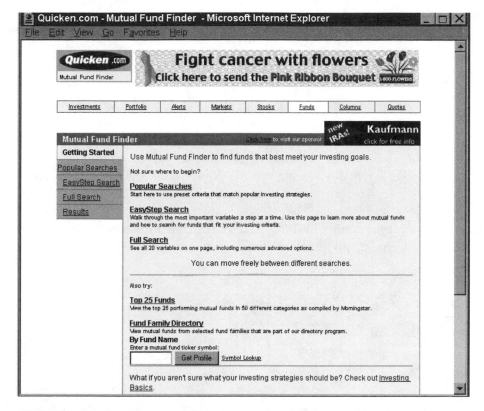

**FIGURE 7.7** Quicken.com offers several levels of mutual fund searches: 11 preset searches, an EasyStep search that takes you step-by-step through the process, and a full search with 20 variables. (Reprinted with permission of Intuit, Inc. Quicken.com is a trademark of Intuit, Inc.)

## *Quicken.com*

Quicken.com's best mutual fund feature is its Mutual Fund Finder (www.quicken.com—Figure 7.7). Preset screens use the Morningstar database to screen funds in several categories: Morningstar's Best; Best of the No-Load, Low Expense Funds; Best Small Funds; Best of the Market Cap Segments; and Best Getting Started Funds (these are funds with low minimum investment). You can also search for the top 25 funds in any of 44 categories, or do a custom search with 20 variables.

Quicken offers both Morningstar and Value Line profiles, and a slew of recycled articles from Mutual Funds Interactive and S&P's Personal-

Wealth.com. If you want to talk about funds, check out the fund forums and message boards in the Talk Back! section.

## Quote.com

Quote.com (www.quote.com) aims to please both Morningstar and Lipper fans by offering profiles and screens from both.

The simple custom screening lets you search for such things as the best funds in a bear or bull market and allows you to weight each criterion as to its importance in the search (Figure 7.8). The advanced screening gives you two preset screens to get you started: the Lipper profile and the Morningstar profile.

The Lipper profile looks for Growth and Income funds with consistent management and high five-year performance with low expense ratios.

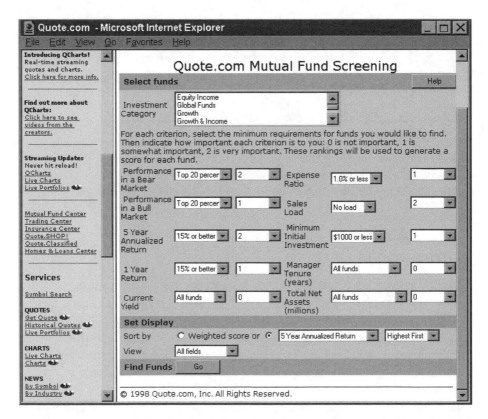

**FIGURE 7.8** Search for funds that perform best in a bear or bull market at Quote.com. (Reprinted with permission of Quote.com.)

The Morningstar profile looks for high-performing, highly rated funds with average or lower risk that invest in large, mostly technology, companies. You can run the screen as is or modify it to suit your own investing strategy. You can also design your own screen profile and save it for future use. The screening is free, but the number of profiles you can save depends on the level of your subscription.

**Lipper Ratings**   Lipper rates a fund based on its performance against similar funds in three market phases: current market, the last up market, and the last down market. This is the Performance Quintile rating. It also rates the fund against all other funds for the same three market phases, which is called the Universal Performance Quintile. Rankings are 1 to 5; the top quintile ranking of 1 means the fund's performance was in the top 20 percent during that market phase.

## SmartMoney.com

SmartMoney.com, a Dow Jones site, has a packed-to-the-brim mutual fund center. Here's a glimpse of its contents.

- ✔ *Funds Today* lists the 10 best funds of the day, along with the date the fund started, its investing strategy, and a brief commentary.
- ✔ *Fund Analyzer* ranks your specified funds by any of 11 criteria, including returns, expense ratios, and SmartMoney grade.

**SmartMoney Grades**   SmartMoney grades a fund from A to F, based on its assessment of the fund's reward-to-risk ratio, allowing for any negative impact of sales charges, annual expenses, and portfolio turnover. Funds are compared to other funds with similar investment objectives. Funds with less than two years of returns are not graded. The top 15 percent are rated A, the next 20 percent B, the middle 30 percent C, the next 20 percent D, and the last 15 percent F.

✔ *Fund Insight* is an in-depth look by SmartMoney analysts at a fund or a stock held by a fund.

✔ *Fund Snapshot* is an abbreviated profile of a fund.

✔ *Fund Finder* is an easy-to-use screening feature (Figure 7.9) that lets you specify some 25 criteria, plus search all funds or specific fund families.

## Thomson Investors Network

Thomson Investors Network (www.thomsoninvest.net) has one of the best prospecting tools for funds: a monthly listing of the top-performing funds in about 48 categories. Market analysis and commentary on funds (by CDA/Weisenberger analysts) is a weekly and monthly staple. Then there is the usual: a fund report (six pages of charts, tables, and graphs); fund alerts; a screening feature; and *net asset value (NAV)* charts. Thomson just lowered its subscription price from $7.95 a month to $34.95 a year.

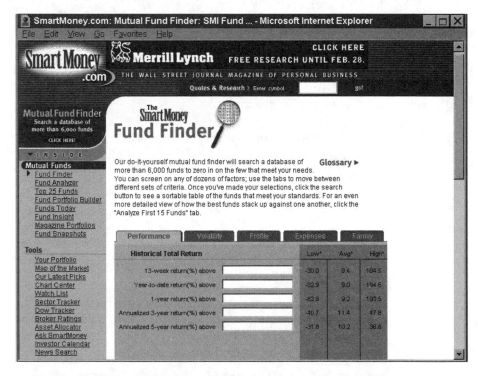

**FIGURE 7.9**  SmartMoney.com has an easy-to-use Fund Finder. (Reprinted with permission of SmartMoney. SmartMoney is a joint publishing venture of Dow Jones & Company, Inc. and The Hearst Corporation.)

## Wall Street City

Wall Street City (www.wallstreetcity.com) has applied the Telescan Pro-Search engine to mutual funds to create one of the more versatile customized mutual funds searches on the Net, and now offers it free to all viewers. You can enter up to 30 variables in a search request, including performance in up markets and down markets. The search report not only lists the top funds to match your screen, but it also displays a graph that shows you how well that search would have performed in the past.

There are also lists of mutual fund searches that are working best (and worst) in the current market. To find them, select What's Working Now from the "Select a Center" drop-down menu; then select Best Searches under Mutual Funds.

## SITES WITH NOTEWORTHY FUND FEATURES

Some sites offer periodic features or special tools for your mutual fund arsenal. Check these out:

- ✔ *The Armchair Millionaire.* This site (www.armchairmillionaire. com) has a mutual fund section called Fund-amentals (Figure 7.10). It features articles, chat rooms, message boards, and a model portfolio. Be sure to check the article archives for an article entitled "Top 10 Mutual Fund Myths," which debunks common misconceptions about mutual funds.

- ✔ *Barron's Online* and *The Wall Street Journal Interactive Edition.* These sister publications pool their resources to bring you a quarterly review of mutual funds. One of Dow Jones's few free offerings, the review is packed with articles and dozens of lists and fund rankings. Check it out at the beginning of each quarter at www.barrons.com or www.wsj.com.

- ✔ *The SEC's EDGAR Filings.* Like public companies, mutual funds are required by the Securities and Exchange Commission to make quarterly and annual filings. You can download these free of charge at the SEC site at www.sec.gov.

- ✔ *Forbes. Forbes* magazine's annual mutual fund survey is now available online (and updated frequently) at www.forbes.com. Two particularly helpful features are the graded domestic and foreign stock funds and the Lipper fund indexes. Each of the 59 Lip-

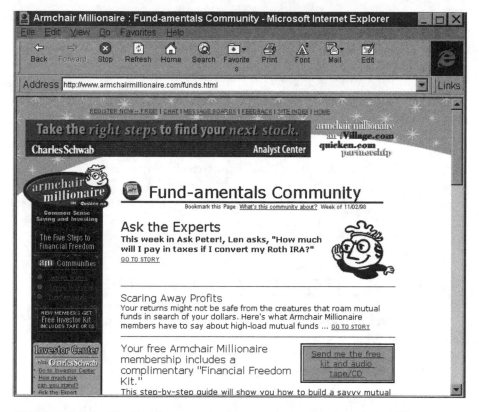

**FIGURE 7.10** The Fund-amentals Community at the Armchair Millionaire offers chat rooms, message boards, articles, and a model portfolio. (Reprinted with permission of Armchair Millionaire.)

per indexes contains 10 to 30 of the largest funds for a particular investment objective category. These can be used not only to judge the best group but as benchmarks for comparing your own portfolio performance.

**The Forbes Grading System**    Forbes assigns letter grades of A+ to F to funds based on their performance in bull markets (up rating) and bear markets (down rating). A fund's performance is ranked against funds with similar investment objectives.

✔ *INVESTools.* This site (www.investools.com) has a Morningstar screen that can filter for a minimum Morningstar rating, a minimum annual return and yield, and a specific investment objective. The search is free; a Morningstar report costs $5.

✔ *Kiplinger.com.* If you want to know the top-performing funds in various categories over the past five years, check out the Top Funds listings at Kiplinger.com (www.kiplinger.com).

✔ *Mutual Fund Café.* This site (www.mfcafe.com) bills itself as a meeting place for mutual fund business and marketing professionals, but even nonprofessionals might find the conversations with industry professionals (called Top Bananas) of interest. It's free.

✔ *TheStreet.com.* This site (www.thestreet.com) has a good fund section that includes lots of archived articles, a weekly forum on funds and one on taxes, and the scoop on fund managers ("Who's Got Your Money?"). To see a list of articles, use the search feature with the keywords "who's got your money." This is a premium feature.

✔ *Value Line.* The best reason to visit Value Line (www.valueline.com) is an online overview called "A Lesson in Mutual Funds" and the 68-page mutual fund guide that you can download and print with the *Adobe Acrobat Reader*. Both are free.

✔ *Yahoo! Finance.* Go to Yahoo! Finance (www.quote.yahoo.com) for free mutual fund news and message boards.

## THE FUND FAMILIES

Fund family Web sites are very much alike in content. Each family wants you to buy its funds, so they offer easy access to fund information including daily NAV prices, fund profiles, and online prospectuses. An increasing number of families offer account access over the Web, automatic investment plans, free exchange privileges among the funds in the family, and the trading of shares online. But the best thing about mutual fund families for the beginning online investor is the carrots.

You remember what carrots are, don't you? The freebies that sites offer to keep you coming back for more, like free portfolio trackers and charts and company snapshots and market news? Well, the carrots offered by mutual fund families include some of the best planning tools and educational materials on the Web.

We lack the space to review even the largest fund families on the Web, so we'll limit ourselves here to a rundown of the best educational offerings. A comparative list of 40 major fund families can be found at CyberInvest.com (www.cyberinvest.com).

## The Vanguard Group

The Vanguard Online University (www.vanguard.com) currently offers two highly structured online courses, with more planned. One is called "The Fundamentals of Mutual Funds" and the other is a "Retirement Investing Seminar" (Figure 7.11). Each course is divided into multiple topics with four to nine lessons on each topic. In addition, Vanguard has an

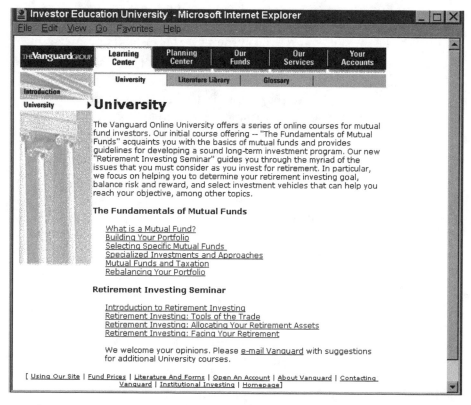

**FIGURE 7.11** The Vanguard Group offers online courses for mutual fund investors. (Copyright © 1998 The Vanguard Group. All rights reserved. Used with permission.)

excellent glossary and a Literature Library where you can read dozens of investing articles online or download them for home study.

## Strong Funds

The Strong Group (www.strongfunds.com) has an excellent learning center, with sections on the Roth IRA, retirement planning, a reference center on the basics of mutual fund investing, and planning tools and calculators. It has gone one step further than most mutual funds, however, and created a separate Web site called EducationIRA.com (www.educationira.com—Figure 7.12). Just about everything you need to know about planning for a child's education can be found there.

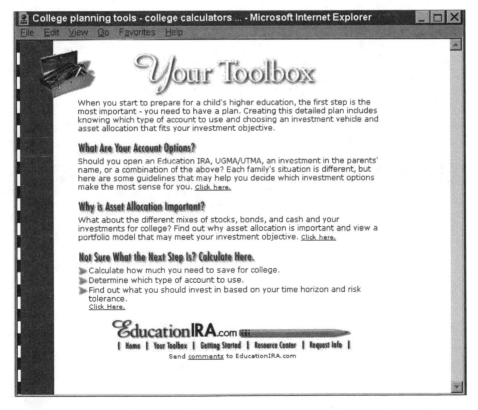

**FIGURE 7.12** EducationIRA.com is a treasure trove of planning tools for children's education, from Strong Funds. (Copyright © 1996–1999 Strong Capital Management, Inc. Reprinted with permission.)

### Stein Roe and Farnham

Stein Roe and Farnham (www.steinroe.com) has a good library of articles and the usual planning tools, but its outstanding educational feature is one for kids: the Young Investor's Fund. (The fund, by the way, carries the highest Morningstar rating.) Buy the fund for a child and he or she will receive educational materials aimed at young investors, including an owner's manual, activity book, and a quarterly newsletter.

### Dreyfus Funds

Dreyfus Online (www.dreyfus.com) has a "Guide to Investing in Uncertain Markets" that should be required reading for today's markets!

## SUMMARY

The mutual fund segment of online investing is expanding rapidly. Dedicated mutual fund sites are proliferating, supersites are beefing up their mutual fund sections, and fund families are awash in new tools and helpful articles. And it's all yours for the clicking.

## WEB SITES FOR MUTUAL FUND INFORMATION

| | |
|---|---|
| Adobe, Inc. | www.adobe.com |
| American Association of Individual Investors (AAII) | www.aaii.com |
| Armchair Millionaire | www.armchairmillionaire.com |
| Barron's Online | www.barrons.com |
| Brill's Mutual Funds Interactive | www.fundsinteractive.com |
| Calvert Group | www.calvertgroup.com |
| CBS MarketWatch | cbs.marketwatch.com/news/newsroom.htx |
| CyberInvest.com | www.cyberinvest.com |
| Dreyfus Funds | www.dreyfus.com |

| | |
|---|---|
| EducationIRA.com | www.educationira.com |
| Fidelity Investments | www.fidelity.com |
| Forbes | www.forbes.com |
| INVESTools | www.investools.com |
| Kiplinger.com | www.kiplinger.com |
| Morningstar.Net | www.morningstar.net |
| Mutual Fund Café | www.mfcafe.com |
| Mutual Fund Investor's Center | www.mfea.com |
| Mutual Funds Online | www.mfmag.com |
| PersonalWealth.com | www.personalwealth.com |
| Quicken.com | www.quicken.com/investments/ mutual funds |
| Quote.com | www.quote.com |
| RealAudio | www.realaudio.com |
| Charles Schwab & Co. | www.schwab.com |
| Securities and Exchange Commission | www.sec.gov |
| SmartMoney.com | www.smartmoney.com |
| Stein Roe and Farnham | www.steinroe.com |
| TheStreet.com | www.thestreet.com |
| Strong Funds | www.strongfunds.com |
| Thomson Investors Network | www.thomsoninvest.net |
| Value Line | www.valueline.com |
| Vanguard Group | www.vanguard.com |
| Wall Street City | www.wallstreetcity.com |
| The Wall Street Journal Interactive Edition | www.wsj.com |
| Yahoo! Finance | www.quote.yahoo.com |

# The FYI Chapter
## Bonds, Options, Futures, and the Global Market

A  s a beginning stock investor, you may think bonds are for the faint of heart and options and futures for wild speculators or the pros. And as for global investing, well! In the current global economic turmoil some might consider it downright suicidal. But the Internet itself is global, and we would be remiss not to at least visit some of its more exotic ports of call.

For those who have longed to expand their investing horizons beyond domestic stocks and mutual funds, this chapter's for you. Everyone else can sample it at their leisure.

Our first stop is bonds.

## BONDS ON THE NET

A *bond* is a security that represents the debt of the entity issuing the bond—federal, state, or local governments, corporations, mortgage companies, and others—rather than ownership in a company. As a bond investor, you are in effect lending money to that entity in exchange for a fixed rate of interest.

Because of its fixed income, many individual investors consider bonds too conservative for words. But there are times when bonds should represent a portion of every investor's portfolio. For example, when interest rates are very high, the projected returns of long-term bonds are quite attractive. And when the risk for equity securities is extremely high, bonds—especially short-term bonds—may represent a safe harbor in a storm.

In any case, we are talking about buying and holding bonds for several years—typically, buying long-term bonds with maturity dates of 5 to 30 years. We are not suggesting that you use bonds as a speculative instrument. Trading bonds, interest rate futures, or other interest rate derivatives is the realm of the professional and the speculator and beyond the scope of this book.

Nonetheless, the wise investor should at least learn how bonds might fit into his or her portfolio. With the Internet, that information is at your fingertips. The purpose of this section is to show you where you can learn about bonds.

## InvestinginBonds.com

"An Investor's Guide to Bond Basics," the online brochure at Investingin-Bonds.com (www.investinginbonds.com), is an excellent source for the novice bond investor. This is the educational site of the Bond Market Association (Figure 8.1). It includes discussions on U.S. *government securities, municipal bonds, corporate bonds, mortgage- and asset-backed securities, federal agency securities,* and *foreign government bonds.* There is also a seven-step checklist for getting started in bonds.

**Corporate Bonds**    Debt obligations issued by private and public corporations; compare with shares of stocks issued by corporations, which are equity instruments.

**Mortgage- and Asset-Backed Securities**    Securities that hold mortgages or other assets, such as buildings, real estate, or corporate notes.

## Bonds Online

Much of Bonds Online (www.bondsonline.com) is aimed at professional bond traders and priced accordingly, but there are two noteworthy free-

**FIGURE 8.1**    The home page of the Bond Market Association's InvestinginBonds.com. (Copyright © 1998 The Bond Market Association. Reprinted with permission.)

bies. One is the Bond Professor, who answers bond-related questions from users. The other is the Economic Statistics Briefing Room (ESBR).

**Federal Agency Securities**    Debt securities issued by Fannie Mae, Freddie Mac, Sallie Mae, Connie Lee, and others—otherwise known as, respectively, the Federal National Mortgage Association, the Federal Home Loan Mortgage Corporation, the Student Loan Marketing Association, the College Construction Loan Insurance Association, and others.

The ESBR provides a unique slant on *leading economic indicators*, which are closely watched by bond investors. (Economic statistics have a more immediate effect on bond rates than on other investment vehicles.) Although many sites offer schedules of release dates, the ESBR takes the reports from various federal agencies and puts them all under one roof, so to speak (Figure 8.2). To get to the ESBR, click Treasuries on the navigation bar, then Economic Indicators. Then click on a link to display the report, or click on the agency's name to go to its Web site.

**Leading Economic Indicators** Statistical reports issued by the U.S. government that indicate the condition of the economy. Some leading economic indicators are unemployment, productivity, housing starts, disposable personal income, gross domestic product, retail sales, and the consumer price index.

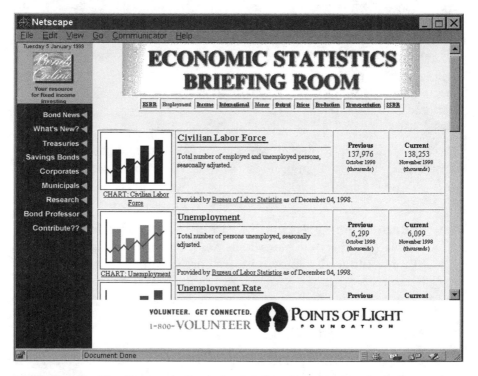

**FIGURE 8.2** The Economic Statistics Briefing Room at Bonds Online gathers government economic reports under one roof. (Reprinted with permission of Bonds Online.)

## And Consider These . . .

Many investing supersites and news sites offer good bond sections. The best ones include:

✔ *Bloomberg.* Bloomberg is one of the major providers of bond news and data. However, the important material is reserved for professional clients who also subscribe to the Bloomberg terminal. About all that's published bond-wise on the Bloomberg Web site (www.bloomberg.com) is the U.S. Treasury yield curve and national municipal bond yields.

✔ *Briefing.com.* This site (www.briefing.com), which won Dow Jones's highest rating as a bond site, is packed with bond news and prices (Figure 8.3). Live bond market commentary, rapid analysis of economic releases, and in-depth coverage of fixed-income markets are part of its professional-level subscription at $25 a month.

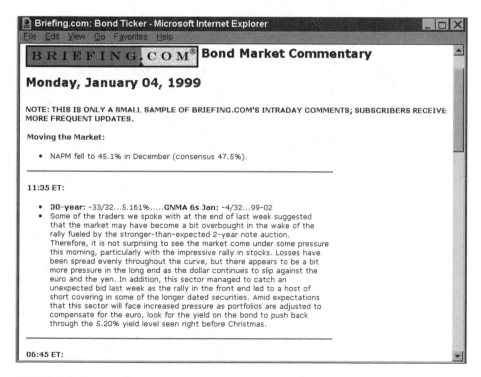

**FIGURE 8.3** Bond market commentary is posted three times a day at Briefing.com. (Reprinted with permission of Briefing.com.)

✔ *Equity Analytics.* This free site (www.e-analytics.com) has good articles on all types of bonds.

✔ *PersonalWealth.com.* The free bond section at www.personal wealth.com offers an economic calendar, a daily brief (from *Business Week*) of important economic reports, a weekly report on the credit world, and a daily Treasury market watch that tracks key interest rates and analyzes the Treasury market. (Click News/Research, then Bonds.) There is also a bond search if you know the name or ticker symbol of the bond.

✔ *Quote.com.* This site (www.quote.com) offers a subscription to bond pricing, which includes quotes on *Treasury bills (T-bills)*, *Treasury notes (T-notes)*, and *Treasury bonds (T-bonds)*, government agency securities, and some 500 other instruments. (Click Bonds on left navigation bar.) The cost is $9.95/month in addition to Quote.com's basic subscription of $9.95/month.

✔ *Reuters Moneynet.* This site (www.moneynet.com) uses pull-down menus to categorize its news. First select Category News on the home page; then scroll to the bottom of the page to see the pull-down menus. For bonds, first select a broad category, such as U.S. Government News, then a subcategory, such as Federal Reserve Watch, U.S. Treasuries, or Municipal Bonds.

✔ *SmartMoney.com.* SmartMoney.com (www.smartmoney.com) has a good bond primer, a bond allocation work sheet, a glossary, and several articles on the risk factor of bonds. But the must-read piece is "The Ten Things Your Broker Won't Tell You about Bonds." (Click Bond Investing on the left navigation bar; then select the article from the pull-down menu.)

✔ *The Syndicate.* If you want to know the ABCs of those Moody bond ratings, you can find the definitions at The Syndicate (www.moneypages.com/syndicate/bonds), along with articles on *bond swaps* and *Treasury auctions*.

✔ *Thomson Investors Network.* Check out www.thomsoninvest.com for an in-depth look at municipal bonds (click Resources). Thomson also has weekly articles on the municipal bond market and a forum on bonds, all part of the $34.95/year site subscription.

**Bond Swaps** A municipal bond investment strategy that lets you take a tax loss and adjust your bond portfolio for credit quality and maturities to meet market considerations and your personal needs. Also called tax swap.

> **Treasury Auctions**   Regularly scheduled public auctions held by the U.S. Department of the Treasury which allow you to buy T-bills, T-bonds, and T-notes directly from the government (if you have a Treasury Direct account, which you can set up through your local Federal Reserve Bank). Check the Treasury Department's Web site for the schedule (www.treas.gov/domfin/auction.htm).

## Bond Brokers

If you want to place your own bond trades, choose an online broker who trades this security. More than a dozen of the 30-plus brokers listed on the broker guide at CyberInvest.com accepts bond trades, although not all brokers trade all types of bonds.

If you want a little more hand-holding, check out these full-service brokers/investment banks:

- ✔ *Salomon Smith Barney* (www.smithbarney.com) has a good bond section, especially for municipals.
- ✔ *Lebenthal & Co.* (www.lebenthal.com) offers a Municipal Bond Information Kit for filling out a short online survey.
- ✔ *First Miami Securities* (www.firstmiami.com) specializes in tax-free bonds.
- ✔ *Stone & Youngberg* (www.styo.com) is a California investment bank that buys and sells municipal bonds and taxable fixed-income securities.

Now, let's take a peek at the wild and woolly world of options and futures.

## OPTIONS AND FUTURES

Options and futures are generally considered sophisticated investment vehicles for professional traders. For the average investor they're much too complicated and speculative. So why put them in an introductory book? Partly because this is an FYI chapter, but also because there are ways the nonprofessional can use them, particularly stock options.

Before we go further, let's define some very general terms.

- ✔ An *option* is a contract that gives you the right but not the obligation to buy or sell a futures contract or a specified quantity of a commodity, security (stock), currency, or index at a specific price within a specified period of time, regardless of the current market price of the underlying item. (From the New York Cotton Exchange glossary.)

✔ *Puts* and *calls* are the purchase and sales instruments for trading options.

**Naked Options**   These are uncovered puts or calls in which the writer does not own the underlying security. Naked options are high-risk because you may in fact be obligated to deliver the security.

**Put**   An option contract that gives the holder the right to sell the underlying security at a specific price for a specific period of time. Puts can be bought or sold.

**Call**   An option contract that gives the holder the right to buy the underlying security at a specific price for a specific period of time. Calls can be bought or sold.

✔ A *futures contract* is a supply contract between a buyer and seller, whereby the buyer is obligated to take delivery and the seller is obligated to provide delivery of a fixed amount of a commodity at a predetermined price at a specified location. Futures contracts are traded exclusively on regulated exchanges and are settled daily based on their current value in the marketplace. (From the New York Mercantile Exchange glossary.)

We'll browse a few futures Web sites, but first, we want to talk about how the average investor can trade stock options for profit and dabble in some low-risk speculation for the sheer fun of it.

### Option Trading for the Beginner

Many conservative investors sell *covered calls* to generate income. That is, they sell *out-of-the-money* calls against stocks they own. If the option remains unexercised on the *expiration date*, they've made the income from selling the call and they still have the stock (the *underlying security*). If the option is called, they have to sell the stock to meet the call, but since they own the stock they have not risked anything. Plus, they still have the extra income from the call. (You can learn more about covered calls in *Getting Started in Options* by Michael C. Thomsett.)

**Out-of-the-Money**   Refers to an option whose strike price is greater (if it is a call) or less (if it is a put) than the current market price of the underlying security.

A relatively low-risk way to trade options is to purchase calls on a stock that appears to be in play—that is, the object of a possible merger or takeover by a major corporation. Such an event is often preceded by unusual volume in the stock's options. If you can track this unusual option activity—and you can with an option search program—you can purchase the calls for a fraction of the price you would pay for the stock. If the merger or acquisition goes through, you can make extraordinary profits for a very small investment. If not—and deals like these do fall through—you've risked relatively little and had some fun doing it. Just be sure that the funds you use for this kind of speculation are truly discretionary.

**Low-Risk Strategy**   This low-risk option strategy of purchasing calls on in-play stocks is described in our *CyberInvesting* book, along with the screen for finding the options.

## Option Quotes and Chains

Many investing supersites offer resources for stock and index options.

✔ *Quote.com* has option quotes, *option chains*, screens, and analyses of the most commonly used option trading strategies.

**Option Chain**   A list of all tradable options on a given stock.

- ✔ *Reuters Moneynet* has option quotes and option chains.
- ✔ *Thomson Investors Network* has free real-time option quotes.
- ✔ *CBS MarketWatch* has option quotes along with a handy list of *expiration month codes*.

**Expiration Month Codes**  The month in which the right to exercise a particular option expires; each month has a code which becomes part of the ticker symbol for that option.

- ✔ *Wall Street City* has option chains, graphs, and an option search product that can be used for finding high-volume calls. The option search feature is part of the $19.95/month site subscription.

Before you even consider trading options, however, you should arm yourself with knowledge—lots of it. The rest of this section will show you where on the Web to find educational resources for options and futures.

## The Exchanges

Based on their educational materials, a primary goal of the options and futures exchanges seems to be to educate the investor.

- ✔ *The Chicago Board Options Exchange.* The CBOE site (www. cboe.com) has everything from introductory material to strategy discussions to options calculators and a symbols directory (Figure 8.4).
- ✔ *The Chicago Board of Trade.* The CBOT site (www.cbot.com) lets you practice trading futures in real time for 30 days without risk, although it will cost you $9.95 or $19.95 depending on the kind of contracts you want to trade. CBOT is also developing online seminars and tutorials, which may be available by the time you read this book.
- ✔ *The Chicago Mercantile Exchange.* For a quick overview of futures and options, try the CME's "Web Instant Lessons" (www.cme.com). These are one-page overviews of such topics as the futures contract, risk management, the trading pit, speculat-

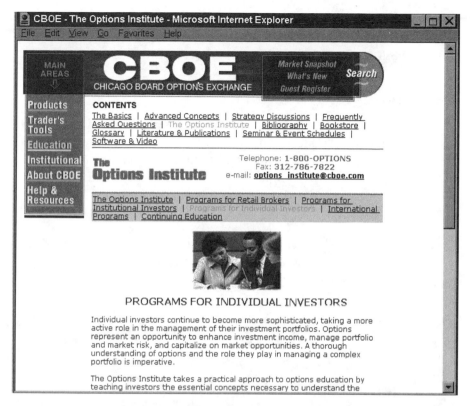

**FIGURE 8.4** The Chicago Board Options Exchange offers educational programs for individual investors through The Options Institute. (Reprinted with permission of the Chicago Board Options Exchange.)

ing and hedging, and options on futures. For further study, the CME offers an "Introduction to Futures," which comes with quizzes, assignments, and final exams, plus a bulletin board and e-mail address for interaction with instructors. The cost is $99. An Introduction to Options course is in the works.

✔ *The Kansas City Board of Trade.* This site (www.kcbt.com) also offers simulated trading of futures and options for a small documentation fee. If you want to advertise your prowess as a trader, check out the KCBT's gift shop where you can purchase sweatshirts, baseball caps, and golf balls with the KCBT logo.

✔ *The Minneapolis Grain Exchange.* This site (www.mex.com) has a series of articles on trading futures, written by its senior economist David W. Bullock. And if you've secretly longed to trade shrimp futures, be sure to read the tutorial on the subject.

✔ *The New York Cotton Exchange* and *The New York Mercantile Exchange.* These two sites (www.nyce.com and www.nymex.com) both have good glossaries of options and futures trading terms.

## The Futures Network

The Futures Network (www.futuresnetwork.com) is an "educational resource for traders, investors, and educators." Most of its content is from the various exchanges, but it offers online simulated trading of futures (in conjunction with AudiTrade) and links to commodity exchanges worldwide. The cost for simulated trading is a $50 setup fee and $2 per trade.

## Futures Online

Futures Online (www.futuresmag.com) is the electronic version of *Futures* magazine (Figure 8.5). You can search past issues for educational articles

**FIGURE 8.5** Futures Online is the online edition of *Futures* magazine. (Reprinted with permission of *Futures* magazine, 250 S. Wacker Dr., #1150, Chicago, IL 60606, 312-977-0999.)

in the Library or buy books and videos in the Learning Center. But the best reason to bookmark this site is the extensive links to other futures and options sites, including a long list of futures brokerage firms. It offers AudiTrack's simulated trading competition for $9.95/month and $0.95/trade.

## INO Global Markets

Known as the Web Center for Futures and Options, this site at www.ino.com (Figure 8.6) acts as a *portal* to other options and futures sites. Some are free; some are not. Among the offerings:

✔ *QuoteWatch.com* (www.quotewatch.com) for option chains.

✔ *MarketCenter.com* (www.marketcenter.com) for free headlines and news related to the options and futures industry.

✔ *GlobalCharts.com* (www.globalcharts.com) for online charting tools for futures and options. Subscription-based.

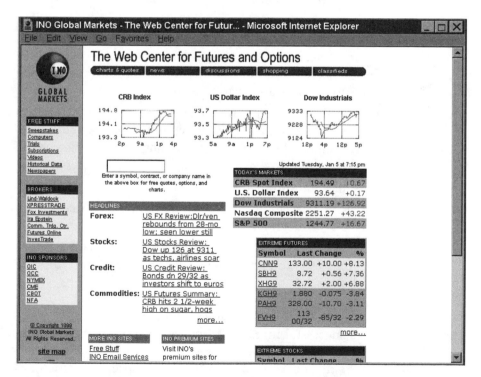

**FIGURE 8.6** The home page of INO Global Markets, the Web Center for Futures and Options. (Reprinted with permission of INO Global Markets.)

✔ *OptionsTrader.com* (www.optionstrader.com) for demos of "power tools" for charting and analyzing options.

✔ *MarketDepot.com* (www.marketdepot.com) for products aimed at traders, such as newsletters and books; analytical, charting, and data products; and educational video- and audiotapes.

## And Consider These . . .

✔ *The Usenet Newsgroup for Futures.* The FAQ (frequently asked questions and answers) for the futures newsgroup (misc.invest. futures) can be found at www.ilhawaii.net/~heinsite/FAQs/ futuresfaq.html. (More about newsgroups in the next chapter.)

**Newsgroup FAQs** A newsgroup FAQ sifts through all the comments in a newsgroup and compiles the best questions and answers into a FAQ. It will save you a lot of time to read the FAQ before you visit the group.

✔ *Commodity Brokers Directory.* This site (www.findbrokers.com) links to commodities brokers by specialty or by state and also has good links to other futures sites.

✔ *AltaVest Worldwide Trading, Inc.* The Futures Learning Center at www.altavest.com has a good introduction to options and futures trading. There is also free online paper trading with real-time prices.

✔ *Lind-Waldock.* This site (www.lind-waldock.com) bills itself as the largest discount futures brokerage.

✔ *First American Discount Corporation.* This site (www.fadc.com) has a nice trading demo.

✔ *Linnco Futures Group of Chicago.* You can download LeoWeb software that lets you trade over the Internet from this site (www.lfgllc.com).

Options and futures are not for everyone. You can completely ignore them and still be a successful investor. Ignoring global markets, however, is a different story. What happens in some small corner of Asia, for example, or Europe or South America, can dramatically impact domestic markets. Regardless of whether you become a global investor, you should be aware of what is happening in markets around the world. We'll show you where to look.

# GLOBAL INVESTING

In the wake of the recent global economic chaos, global investing has lost its luster for many investors. And even in the best of times, it is not for everyone. But it is important to be aware of global market activity for the simple reason that what happens in those markets creates ripples and often spasms in our own. That's why no book on online investing would be complete without a few words about the myriad global investing resources on the Internet.

**Country Funds**   For the average investor, the best way to participate in the global market is to invest in *country funds*. These are mutual funds that buy stocks of companies in a particular country or region. Most large fund families offer one or more country funds (see Chapter 7).

We'll look first at some general investing sites that offer resources for the global investor. Then we'll introduce you to major investing sites in key countries.

## *Bloomberg*

Bloomberg (www.bloomberg.com) works hard to keep you abreast of global market news. It has headlines and summaries from major world newspapers and a recap of news-making stocks in the United Kingdom and Japan. Of particular interest is the update on the *European Monetary Union (EMU)*, and links to Web sites that offer more information on the EMU. Bloomberg also dedicates entire Web sites to Australia and New Zealand (Figure 8.7), Germany, Italy, Japan, Latin America, and the U.K., all of which can be reached through links on the Bloomberg home page. Unfortunately for English-only speakers, the German, Italian, and Japanese sites are in the language of the country.

## *Bridge Information Services*

Global investors will want to bookmark Bridge (www.bridge.com) for its summary of major world indexes (under Market Data) (Figure 8.8).

Similar summaries can be viewed for the Americas, European, and Asian markets. Not much is free at this site, but the dedicated global investor may want to subscribe to BridgeNews, which provides concise,

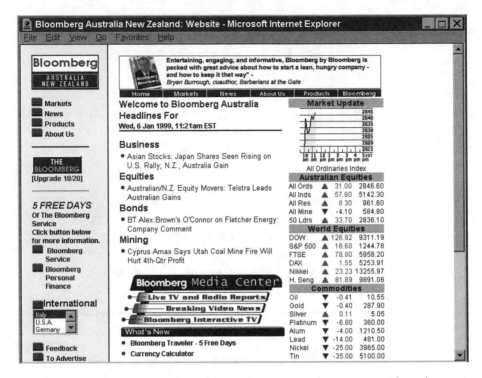

**FIGURE 8.7** The home page of Bloomberg Australia. (Source: Bloomberg. Reprinted with permission.)

comprehensive previews of the day's economic events for nearly 40 countries. Other subscription-based products include in-depth articles, interviews, data feeds, and surveys on global economic issues such as the Asian financial crisis.

### *InterMoney*

InterMoney (www.intermoney.com) offers commentary on the short-term and long-term outlook for global markets and the world economy (Figure 8.9). It also has *foreign exchange rates* for *currency conversion*; country profiles for Canada, Europe, Asia, and Latin America; a report on the European Monetary Union; and a glossary of financial market terms. The site is free, but registration is required.

### *And Consider These . . .*

These sites have global investing features of particular interest:

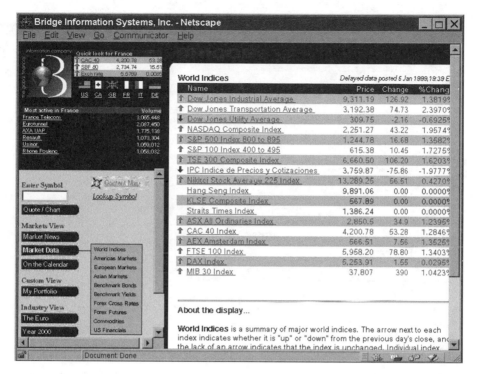

**FIGURE 8.8** Bridge's World Indices provides a quick comparison of world markets. (Reprinted with permission of Bridge Information Systems, Inc.)

✔ *Ernst & Young International.* The Doing Business In . . . guides at Ernst & Young International (www.eyi.com) offer guidance for investing in foreign countries.

✔ *The Fortune Global 500.* This site (www.pathfinder.com/fortune/global500) is a list of the top 500 international companies, along with a company snapshot of each.

✔ *The Global Investor.* (www.global-investor.com) has a good directory for global investing sites and a listing of international *American Depositary Receipts (ADRs)* issued in the United States. A feature called the Q-Links Panel displays equity, interest rate, currency, and commodity charts for major world markets. Free.

✔ *I/B/F/S Financial Network.* This site (www.ibes.com) is noteworthy for its earnings estimates and research on 18,000 stocks in 52 countries. The global service is $49.95/month for 25 companies or $249.95/month for 150 companies.

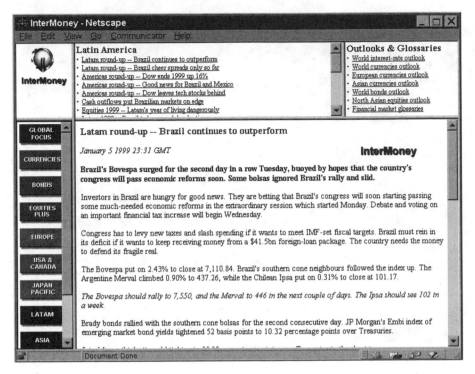

**FIGURE 8.9** InterMoney provides stats and commentary on world markets. (Reprinted with permission of I.D.E.A.)

✔ *The Wall Street Journal Interactive Edition.* The Journal (www.wsj.com) reports the news on Asia, Europe, and the Americas and publishes special reports from time to time on global investing. Subscription: $29/year for print subscribers; $59/year for nonprint subscribers.

✔ *Yahoo! Finance.* Yahoo! Finance (www.quote.yahoo.com) has country-specific sites, in the language of the country. Current global Yahoos! include: United Kingdom and Ireland, Australia and New Zealand, France, Germany, Italy, Spain, Denmark, Norway, Sweden, Korea, China, and Japan. By the time you read this, there will no doubt be more.

✔ *ZDNet Inter@ctive Investor.* The site (www.zdii.com) offers a snapshot of global market activity with its ZDII Global index, a global technology index that tracks the performance of 30 Asian, 30 European, and 40 North American companies. There are also separate indexes for Asia, Europe, and North America. Free.

### Country-Specific Sites

Because the Internet is global, you can go directly to Web sites in the country of your choice for investing and economic data. Here are a few to get you started. All are free.

### Asia

- ✔ *Asia, Inc.* (www.asia-inc.com) is a site you can bookmark for the Asia Internet Directory, a search engine that focuses on Asian and business resources.

- ✔ *AsiaOne* (www.asia1.com.sg) covers Singapore and Kuala Lumpur.

- ✔ *The Business Times Singapore Online* (biztimes.asia1.com) is an excellent way to stay abreast of Asian markets (Figure 8.10).

**FIGURE 8.10** The home page of the Business Times Singapore Online. (Reprinted with permission of Singapore Press Holdings.)

✔ *Inside China Today* (www.insidechina.com). News and online news from China.

✔ *Interactive Investor International—Asia* (www.iii-asia.com). Comprehensive investing site, mostly in English. Hong Kong–approved funds (some in Chinese) and more. Links to other Interactive Investor International sites (United Kingdom, Offshore, and South Africa).

## Australia

✔ *The Australian News Network* (www.theaustralian.com.au). All the Australian news that's fit for cyberspace. Check out the Business section.

✔ *Macquarie On-Line* (www.macquarie.com.au). The Macquarie Bank site with hourly currency updates and more.

## Canada

✔ *Canada Newswire* (www.newswire.ca). Full-text news release service, the Canadian equivalent of PR Newswire.

✔ *Canadian Online Explorer* (www.canoe.ca/MoneyStocks/home. html) (Figure 8.11). Canadian and U.S. stock quotes, market highlights, news, and mutual funds.

✔ *The Globe and Mail* (www.theglobeandmail.com). "Canada's National Newspaper" now online. Links to related sites: Globe-Fund.com (everything you wanted to know about Canadian mutual funds) and Globetechnology.com (the last word on high-tech companies).

## The Caribbean

✔ *Caribbean Online* (www.caribbeanonline.com) is the place to learn about investing in the Caribbean Islands, from the Florida Keys to Venezuela, and it includes listings for hotels, companies, and organizations.

## Europe

✔ *Europe Online* (www.europeonline.com) is a portal to European Web sites (Figure 8.12). Click the country of your choice, then Business and Finance. EuroSeek is a country-specific search engine that can be viewed in more than 30 different languages.

**FIGURE 8.11** This is the Market Watch page of Canadian Online Explorer (CANOE). (Reprinted with permission of CANOE.)

✔ *FT.com* (www.ft.com) is the Web site of the *Financial Times*, a leading international English-language business newspaper.

✔ *Central Europe Online* (www.centraleurope.com) provides business news and country information on Poland, the Czech Republic, Slovakia, Hungary, Slovenia, and Romania.

✔ *SwissInvest.com* (www.swissinvest.com) provides information on Swiss stocks, financial instruments, financial services, reports, research, and investments (Figure 8.13).

## Russia

✔ *Interfax Russian News Agency.* (www.interfax-news.com) News and information on Russia, the Commonwealth of Independent States (CIS), and Baltic countries.

✔ *Russia Today.* (www.russiatoday.com) More news on Russia.

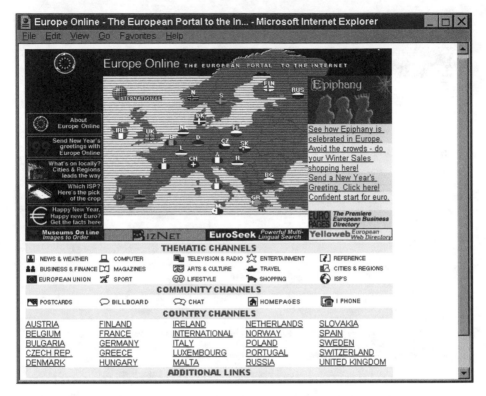

**FIGURE 8.12** Europe Online is a portal to European Web sites, with 25 country channels which can be viewed in English or the language of the country. (Reprinted with permission of Europe Online.)

## South America

✔ *Brazil Financial Wire.* (www.agestado.com/bfw) Economic, political, and financial news on Brazil.

✔ *Peru.com.* (www.peru.com) Industry and economic information for Peru; in English or Spanish.

## Middle East and Africa

✔ *Africa Online.* (www.africaonline.com) News, market updates, business- and finance-related issues, company profiles for the Ivory Coast, Ghana, Kenya, Tanzania, and Zimbabwe, and links to African-related sites.

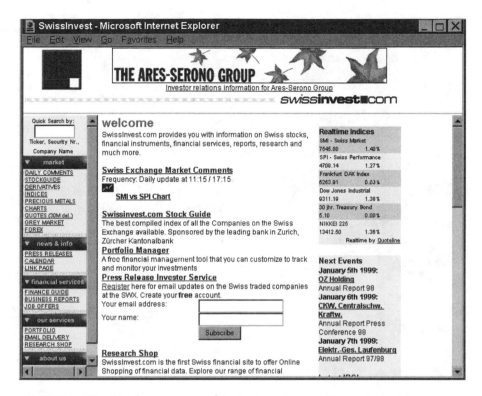

**FIGURE 8.13** The home page of SwissInvest.com. (Reprinted with permission of Swissmedia Center.)

✔ *Africa News Online.* (www.africanews.org) News coverage for all of Africa.

✔ *Arabia.On.Line.* (www.arabiaonline.com) A portal to country Web sites for 16 Middle Eastern countries (Figure 8.14). There's also a search engine dedicated to Arabian Web sites. Available in English or Arabic.

✔ *Israel's Business Arena.* (www.globes.co.il) Business and market news in English or Hebrew.

Regardless of whether you explore the global sites in this section, it is important to pay attention to global events. As the fall of 1998 attested, not to do so is bordering on foolishness. Undoubtedly, global information will become easier to find and assimilate as the world grows even smaller in the next century.

**FIGURE 8.14**  Arabia.On.Line is a gateway to investment opportunities in the Middle East. (Reprinted with permission of Arabia.On.Line.)

## SUMMARY

This chapter, as we said earlier, is for informational purposes only. Bonds, options, futures, and global investing are important to the serious investor, but beginning investors can put them aside until they've become comfortable with domestic equities. In fact, you can rule them out completely and still be a successful investor. We simply want you to be aware of them and know where to go to expand your investing horizons.

## WEB SITES FYI

*Bonds*

| | |
|---|---|
| Bloomberg | www.bloomberg.com |
| Bonds Online | www.bondsonline.com |
| Briefing.com | www.briefing.com |

| | |
|---|---|
| Equity Analytics | www.e-analytics.com |
| First Miami Securities | www.firstmiami.com |
| InvestinginBonds.com | www.investinginbonds.com |
| Lebenthal & Co. | www.lebenthal.com |
| PersonalWealth.com | www.personalwealth.com |
| Quote.com | www.quote.com |
| Reuters Moneynet | www.moneynet.com |
| Salomon Smith Barney | www.smithbarney.com |
| SmartMoney.com | www.smartmoney.com |
| Stone & Youngberg | www.styo.com |
| The Syndicate | www.moneypages.com/syndicate/bonds |
| Thomson Investors Network | www.thomsoninvest.net |
| U.S. Treasury Dept. | www.treas.gov/domfin/auction.htm |

### Options and Futures

| | |
|---|---|
| Altavest Worldwide Trading | www.altavest.com |
| CBS MarketWatch | cbs.marketwatch/news/newsroom.htx |
| Chicago Board Options Exchange | www.cboe.com |
| Chicago Board of Trade | www.cbot.com |
| Chicago Mercantile Exchange | www.cme.com |
| Commodity Brokers Directory | www.findbrokers.com |
| CyberInvest.com | www.cyberinvest.com |
| First American Discount Brokerage | www.fadc.com |
| The Futures Network | www.futuresnetwork.com |
| Futures Newsgroup FAQ | www.ilhawaii.net/~heinsite/FAQs/futuresfaq.html |
| Futures Online | www.futuresmag.com |
| GlobalCharts.com | www.globalcharts.com |
| INO Global Markets | www.ino.com |

| | |
|---|---|
| Kansas City Board of Trade | www.kcbt.com |
| Lind-Waldock | www.lind-waldock.com |
| Linnco Futures Group of Chicago | www.lfgllc.com |
| MarketCenter.com | www.marketcenter.com |
| MarketDepot.com | www.marketdepot.com |
| Minneapolis Grain Exchange | www.mex.com |
| New York Cotton Exchange | www.nyce.com |
| New York Mercantile Exchange | www.nymex.com |
| OptionsTrader.com | www.optionstrader.com |
| Quote.com | www.quote.com |
| QuoteWatch.com | www.quotewatch.com |
| Reuters Moneynet | www.moneynet.com |
| SmartMoney.com | www.smartmoney.com |
| Thomson Investors Network | www.thomsoninvest.net |
| Wall Street City | www.wallstreetcity.com |

### Global Investing

| | |
|---|---|
| Africa News Online | www.africanews.org |
| Africa Online | www.africaonline.com |
| Arabia OnLine | www.arabiaonline.com |
| Asia, Inc. | www.asia-inc.com |
| AsiaOne | www.asia1.com.sg |
| Australian News Network | www.theaustralian.com.au |
| Bloomberg | www.bloomberg.com |
| Brazil Financial Wire | www.agestado.com/bfw |
| Bridge Information Services | www.bridge.com |
| Business Times Singapore Online | biztimes.asia1.com |
| Canada Newswire | www.newswire.ca |
| Canadian Online Explorer | www.canoe.ca/MoneyStocks/home.html |
| Caribbean Online | www.caribbeanonline.com |

| | |
|---|---|
| CBS MarketWatch | cbs.marketwatch/news/ newsroom.htx |
| Central Europe Online | www.centraleurope.com |
| Ernst & Young International | www.eyi.com |
| Europe Online | www.europeonline.com |
| Fortune Global 500 | www.pathfinder.com/fortune/ global500 |
| FT.com | www.ft.com |
| Global Investor | www.global-investor.com |
| Globe and Mail | www.theglobeandmail.com |
| I/B/E/S Financial Network | www.ibes.com |
| Inside China Today | www.insidechina.com |
| Interactive Investor International-Asia | www.iii-asia.com |
| Interfax Russian News Agency | www.interfax-news.com |
| InterMoney | www.intermoney.com |
| Israel's Business Arena | www.globes.co.il |
| Macquarie On-Line | www.macquarie.com.au |
| Peru.com | www.peru.com |
| Russia Today | www.russiatoday.com |
| Scandinavia Now Online | www.scandinavianowonline.com |
| SwissInvest.com | www.swissinvest.com |
| The Wall Street Journal Interactive Edition | www.wsj.com |
| Yahoo! Finance | www.quote.yahoo.com |
| ZDNet | www.zdnet.com |

*Chapter*

# Nurtured by the Net
## IPOs, DPOs, DRIPs, DSPs, Chats, and Banks

**B**y almost any measure, the Internet is changing the way we do business. Throughout this book we've shown you ways in which the Internet has expanded our access to investing resources. There are several areas, however, that simply would not exist in their current state without an Internet. Some, like initial public offerings (IPOs), dividend reinvestment plans (DRIPs), and online banking have a pre-Internet existence but are greatly enhanced by the Net's vast audience and ease of access. A few, like direct public offerings (DPOs), chat rooms, and message boards, are entirely children of the Net.

The nurturing power of the Internet is the common thread running through the disparate topics of this chapter.

## INITIAL PUBLIC OFFERINGS

What do the names eBay, uBid, and Broadcast.com mean to you?

If you said Internet companies, you'd be right. But they are a very special breed of Internet companies. As initial public offerings (IPOs), each gained more than 100 percent in value from the *opening price* on the day it went public. Although such success stories are the exception rather than the rule, hot issues like these have helped make IPOs the investment topic of the late 1990s. And, with its vast storehouse of information and the ease of online trading, the Internet itself has been a catalyst in bringing IPOs into the realm of the individual investor.

An initial public offering is the process by which a privately owned company sells its shares to the public for the first time. It is a lengthy proceeding strictly governed by the rules and regulations of the Securities and Exchange Commission (SEC). Part of the process is the *due diligence* that the *underwriter* performs to determine if the company is suitable to become a public company. A *selling syndicate* put together by the underwriter establishes a reasonable offering price and assists the company's *aftermarket performance* by writing research reports and creating a supportive environment.

**Due Diligence**   The process of checking a company's background and financial condition in order to deem it worthy of offering its shares to the public in an initial public offering.

**Underwriter**   Called the lead underwriter, this is the investment bank that "takes a company public," performing the due diligence, setting the offering price, putting together the selling syndicate, and generally shepherding the company through the many steps of an initial public offering.

**Aftermarket Performance**   The performance of an IPO after it has begun trading, usually in comparison with the offering price.

IPOs are considered high-risk investments because many do not have any earnings history by which to judge their performance. Many IPOs are young companies that have not had to manage a significant amount of money or meet quarterly performance standards. As a public company it has to do both, and more often than not the company ends up trading below its offering price.

Still, IPOs hold a great attraction for individual investors who hope to find the next eBay or uBid!

If IPOs appeal to you as an investment vehicle, we suggest you read "The ABCs of IPOs" at CBS MarketWatch. This four-part series written by Darren Chervitz and published in August 1998 is the best overview we've seen on the subject. Part 1 is a glossary that identifies such colorful IPO jargon as *red herring* and *greenshoe*. Part 2 takes you through the IPO process; Part 3 tells you what to look for in the prospectus that could signal danger; and Part 4 provides some strategies for investing in an IPO.

**Red Herring**   Nickname for the preliminary prospectus filed in an initial public offering, so called because of the warning, printed in red, that the information in the document is incomplete or subject to change.

**Greenshoe**   In an IPO, this is a percentage of the total underwriting, usually 15 percent, that can be purchased by the underwriters in addition to the scheduled allotment of shares. The greenshoe is usually invoked if the deal is hot or overbooked. It is also called an overallotment.

The article also talks about how to get in on the ground floor of an IPO. This has always been somewhat difficult for an individual investor. The brokers who have access to an IPO—most often investment banks or full-service brokers—usually offer participation only to their biggest and best customers. But that is changing.

The CBS MarketWatch article names three online brokerages that act as distribution channels for IPOs and now offer them to clients: E*Trade (www.etrade.com), Charles Schwab (www.eschwab.com), and Wit Capital (www.witcapital.com). Having an account at one of these firms doesn't necessarily guarantee you a piece of an IPO, but it does increase your chances.

### The Stages of an IPO

IPOs are generally grouped into four classifications at the Web sites that track them:

✔ *Recent Filings.* These are IPOs that have filed their *S-1 registration statements* with the SEC within the past week or so.

✔ *Scheduled Pricings.* The offering price is assigned to the IPO a day or two before it is scheduled to be traded.

✔ *In Registration.* The period from the day a company files its registration statement until 25 days after the stock starts trading is known as the *quiet period.* During this time the company is *in registration* and is forbidden by the SEC to publicize its stock in any way or to say anything not included in the registration statement. This phase encompasses recent filings and scheduled pricings.

✔ *Aftermarket Performance.* This refers to the performance of an IPO's stock any time after it starts trading. Incidentally, insiders who did not sell shares in the IPO are restricted from selling their shares for a period of about 180 days (called the *lock-up period*).

**S-1 Registration Statement** The document filed with the SEC which announces a company's intent to go public. It can be downloaded free at www.sec.gov.

You can track an IPO through its various phases at more than a dozen Web sites that specialize in IPOs and investing supersites that have IPO sections. Here are a few places to get started; then just follow the links.

## IPO Web Sites

The following sites track IPOs in one or all of the four stages. Most have educational resources, though none quite as good as "The ABCs of IPOs" at CBS MarketWatch.

✔ *Hoover's IPO Central.* (www.ipocentral.com) IPO Central offers filings, pricings, alerts, and an aftermarket performance chart (Figure 9.1) that includes offering and opening price with the first day's close. (Click IPO Directory to find it.) In addition, subscribers to Hoover's Online ($12.95/month) can access real-time SEC filings as well as receive e-mail alerts about new filings.

**FIGURE 9.1** The Aftermarket Performance page at Hoover's IPO Central. (Reprinted with permission of Hoover's Online, Austin, Texas; www.hoovers.com. Copyright © 1998.)

✔ *IPO Maven.* (www.ipomaven.com) The best feature here is the IPO Profile. It summarizes the IPO's vital statistics so you don't have to wade through the prospectus until you're ready to buy.

✔ *IPO Intelligence Online.* (www.ipo-fund.com) This site offers IPO news, an IPO pick of the week, an IPO message board, and an IPO mutual fund (Figure 9.2).

✔ *CBS MarketWatch.* (cbs.marketwatch/news/newsroom.htx) Among the IPO offerings here are a Daily Report, First Words (an interview with the CEO after the quiet period has expired), a Pick of the Week, and the previously mentioned "ABC's of IPOs."

✔ *Quicken.com.* (quicken.elogic.com/ipo/index.asp) Quicken tracks all four stages of IPOs, plus it provides a daily list of the top 10 IPO gainers and losers in the aftermarket.

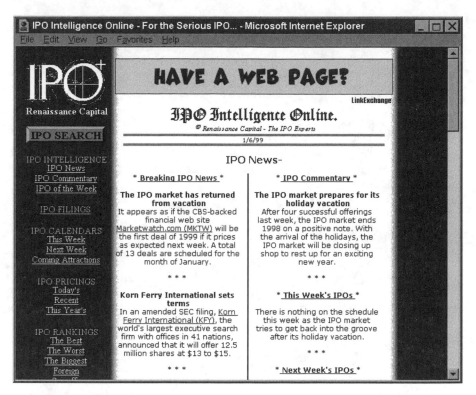

**FIGURE 9.2** The home page of IPO Intelligence Online. (Reprinted with permission of Renaissance Capital.)

✔ *PersonalWealth.com.* (www.personalwealth.com) Among other features, PersonalWealth's IPO section includes IPO picks and pans and a small-cap/IPO model portfolio.

✔ *ZDNet.* (www.zdnet.com) ZDNet's twist on IPOs is the Red Herring IPO 100, an index of the hottest technology IPOs to price within the last 18 months. The site also offers news and commentary, an IPO calendar, and a performance calculator that lets you enter an IPO stock symbol and compare the current price with the first day open, first day close, or offering price.

**IPO Message Boards**  Red Herring at www.redherring. com features IPO message boards.

Now let's look at the kissin' cousin of the IPO: the direct public offering (DPO).

# DIRECT PUBLIC OFFERINGS

Initial public offerings offer investors a chance to get in on the ground floor. Direct public offerings give you a chance to help build the ground floor.

In a direct public offering (DPO) a company foregoes the traditional underwriter and sells its shares directly to the public. The company still has to file an S-1 Registration Statement with the SEC, and it is governed by state regulations, but a DPO is not subject to the process, described earlier, that is imposed on companies going through an underwriter.

Without the underwriter's due diligence and the selling syndicate's pricing and aftermarket support, a DPO is inherently more risky than a traditional IPO. You, the investor, are responsible for conducting your own due diligence, and that is not easy to do. Your only source of information is the SEC document, which you should read very, very carefully. If that doesn't scare you away and if you have a stash of completely disposable funds, then by all means consider DPOs.

**State Regulations** DPOs are unavailable in certain states. This information should be listed on the site offering the DPO.

## The Internet and the DPO

In 1996, Andy Klein, now CEO of Wit Capital, launched the first DPO on the Internet, raising $1.6 million for Spring Street Brewery. Subsequently, he started Wit Capital (www.witcapital.com), one of the discount brokers that distributes traditional IPOs to individual investors. Wit Capital also sponsors direct public offerings (which it calls *public venture capital offerings*), although at this point none are posted on the site.

**The Sophisticated Investor** To view a DPO prospectus or a "private placement memorandum," you must register and acknowledge that you are a "sophisticated investor," which means, in essence, that you understand the nature and risks of the investment.

Other sources for DPO listings are the Emerging Companies Network (www.capital-network.com) and Yahoo! Finance (quote.yahoo.com). Yahoo! Finance calls them *online offerings*, which it posts under Initial Public Offerings.

The DPO Web site with a difference is Direct Stock Market (www. directstockmarket.com). In addition to posting DPOs and private placements, Direct Stock Market offers a trading bulletin board where investors can buy and sell shares of DPOs not only in the initial offering but in the *secondary market* as well (Figure 9.3). The required SEC approval took almost two years, and the trading system was not launched until late 1998, so it is still a fledgling market.

**Secondary Market**    A market in which an investor purchases shares of stocks or other securities from another investor, rather than from the corporation itself. The New York Stock Exchange and NASDAQ are secondary markets. One of the problems with DPOs is there is no readily accessible secondary market.

If the DPO concept has piqued your interest, you can read more about it at Direct Stock Market and The Emerging Companies Network.

Now let's head to the opposite end of the spectrum from DPOs and take a look at the DRIP phenomenon.

## DRIPs, DRPs, DIPs, AND DSPs

*DRIPs*, *DRPs*, *DIPs*, and *DSPs*: These are not put-downs for the lisping creep who sat next to you in your high school English class. They are acronyms that represent an emerging trend in online investing and they have one thing in common: They can give you a way to avoid broker commissions altogether and buy stock directly from a company with little or no fees.

DRIPs and DSPs have become the new kid on the Net, with a DRIP link on every investing supersite. If the idea of stiffing your broker appeals to you—and you consider yourself a long-term investor—read on.

The concept began as dividend reinvestment plans (DRIPs or DRPs), which allowed dividends to be automatically reinvested in a company's stock. Out of that grew the *direct investment plan (DIP)* or *direct stock plan*

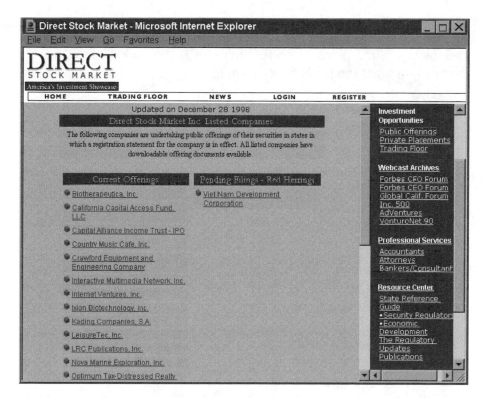

**FIGURE 9.3**  This is a list of direct public offerings at Direct Stock Market on December 28, 1998. (Reprinted with permission of Direct Stock Market.)

*(DSP)* through which shareholders can make small cash investments to buy stock directly from the company. (Many DRIPs also allow for optional cash purchases of stock.)

More than 1100 companies now offer DRIPs and DSPs, including blue chips like AT&T, Exxon, and McDonald's. The only catch is, you must own at least one share of the company's stock and it must be held in your name, as opposed to the *street name*. In the past, that first share had to be purchased through a broker, if you didn't already own the stock. Now, more and more companies are implementing direct stock purchase plans even for the initial purchase.

**Street Name**  Refers to the registered holder of a security when it is held in the broker's name, rather than in the name of the person who owns the stock.

## Advantages and Disadvantages

Before we get into specific Web resources for DRIPs and DSPs, let's review some of their advantages and disadvantages.

### Advantages

✔ You can bypass the broker and avoid commissions on stock trades.

✔ Any fees charged by the company or plan administrator are nominal. The fees seem to be growing, however, so be sure to read the plan carefully.

✔ The initial investment can be small.

✔ Dollar-cost averaging can be achieved with regular cash investments.

### Disadvantages

✔ You have to be a *registered shareholder* in order to enroll in a company-sponsored DRIP/DSP plan. You can buy the first share either through a broker or, in plans that offer *direct enrollment*, directly through the company.

**Direct Enrollment**    A dividend reinvestment plan that allows an individual to purchase stock directly from the company.

✔ The timing of the purchase and sale of shares is determined by the plan administrator, and selling a stock may take five to ten trading days. What this means is that you have no control over the actual price at which stock is bought or sold; as a result, these plans appeal primarily to long-term investors.

If this sounds like you, here are some Internet resources to get you started.

## Learning about DRIPs and DSPs

One of the most extensive collections of articles about DRIPs and DSPs can be found at the DRIP Investor (www.dripinvestor.com). Charles Carlson, editor of the DRIP Investor newsletter, writes a weekly column on DRIPs, and more than 50 of his past columns are archived on his site and at Quicken.com (www.quicken.com/investments). In addition, there is a FAQ that provides straightforward answers to the most basic questions, a list of companies that offer DRIPs and DSPs, and a clearinghouse section where you can request enrollment information from dozens of companies.

PersonalWealth.com has an article on DRIPs called "Building a Portfolio Inexpensively" and a list of companies sponsoring DRIPs. The cool thing about this list is the S&P STARS rankings. If you're looking for DRIPs that are five-star stocks, this is the place to find them. (Click News/Research, then Stocks.)

The MoneyPaper (www.moneypaper.com) is a subscription-based advisory service for DRIP and DSP investors. A free article at the site, "The Dark Side of Direct Enrollment," gives you the lowdown on fees and is a must-read for DRIP investors (click Publications, then DRP Authority).

Stock1.com (www.stock1.com) features an article entitled "DRP Features & Benefits" that enumerates the main points of buying DRIPs in a clear, bulleted list. The article is free, but a list of the 50 Best DRPs costs $10.

DRIP Central (www.dripcentral.com) has articles and a DRIP message board, but mainly there are links, links, and more links to things DRIP-related.

The Motley Fool (www.fool.com) has put together a DRIP portfolio, which includes the research that led to the buy decisions. The Fool also has a couple of message boards devoted to DRIPs.

## Buying DRIPs and DSPs

Once you've done the required reading, go to Netstock Direct (www.netstockdirect.com) to check out its DRIP and DSP plans (Figure 9.4). This site provides detailed plan summaries of U.S. and non-U.S. DRIPs and DSPs. (Non-U.S. companies offer DRIPs though American depositary receipts or ADRs.)

**Kidstock.com**   Check out the link to Kidstock.com. It is designed to teach children about money and investing in general, with special sections on DRIPs and DSPs.

Companies that offer detailed plan summaries and enrollment forms online are noted with an icon; otherwise, you have to call for the informa-

**FIGURE 9.4** Netstock Direct is a major source of DRIP and DSP plans. (Reprinted with permission of Netstock Direct Corporation. Copyright © 1998 Netstock Direct Corporation. All rights reserved.)

tion. Links are provided to the company's Web site, if available, and to research materials from Wall Street Research Network (www.wsrn.com).

An advanced search feature at Netstock Direct lets you screen DSPs and DRIPs by industry, by the stock exchange on which the company is listed, and by 13 other criteria. An electronic enrollment feature is in the works and may be online by the time you read this.

Another required stop for the DRIP investor is First Chicago Trust Company (www.fctc.com), which administers more than 160 *bank-sponsored plans* for some of the bluest of blue-chip companies. In a DSP plan, you can buy your first share of stock directly through First Chicago; in a DRIP plan, you must already own at least one share. Read the FAQ here to learn about the details of signing up.

If you want to commune with other DRIP investors, go to the free message board at www.dripinvestor.com. Which segues nicely into our next topic, the message boards and chat rooms of online communities.

**Bank-Sponsored Plans** A direct stock purchase plan (DSP) or dividend reinvestment plan (DRIP) that is administered by a bank rather than the company itself.

## CHAT ROOMS AND MESSAGE BOARDS

*Netizens* love to talk to other netizens, and every major Web site hosts one or more chat rooms or message boards. Their objective is to build an on-line community to which users will return again and again (building up those page impressions!). A popular gathering place is one of the best ways to ensure return visits.

Investors, who like to talk as much as anyone, will find online communities on virtually every major investing site and at some sites that exist solely for chatting and posting. Most are free, although one of the most popular, Silicon Investor, charges an annual fee if you want to post a message, but lets you read the boards without charge.

We'll point you to some of the best community centers, but let's define a few terms first.

A chat room is conducted in real time. Participants enter a virtual room dedicated to a particular subject. They then communicate by typing a message and hitting Enter. The message, identified by the chatter's nickname, immediately appears on the screen.

Chat rooms can be very chaotic. Multiple chatters carry on "conversations" over the heads, so to speak, of the other chatters, and the screen is peppered with inane and irrelevant comments. We don't care much for unmoderated chat rooms, but we appear to be in the minority.

A message board does not take place in real time. It is more linear in structure, like a bulletin board (as it is also called) with all messages identified by subject, date, and nickname. Participants can post messages on a new topic or reply to a posted message. All replies to a message are linked, creating a *thread* on a particular topic which allows you to follow an entire "conversation."

A *moderated session* can take the form of a live chat or a message board. A moderated chat takes place in real time and features a guest to whom the questions are addressed and a host who manages the sequence of questions and answers. A moderated message board features an expert of whom you can ask questions which are posted and answered in the same manner as any message board.

Every chat room and message board has its rules, regulations, and *netiquette*, posted at the site, that you are expected to follow. Generally speaking, you're prohibited from using profanity and must conduct yourself in a civil manner, refraining from personal attacks on other participants. It's a good idea to read the rules before joining a group. Registration is almost always required, but usually it consists simply of entering your e-mail address and choosing a nickname for yourself.

*A word of warning:* At the risk of repeating ourselves, we caution you to take comments about specific stocks with a grain of salt. With the ability to hide behind a nickname and with no requirement to state their position in a stock, the unscrupulous can hype a stock for their own personal gain or trash a stock out of revenge for some real or imagined slight. The point is: You have no idea of their personal agenda.

That said, let's begin with the Big Four investing communities: Silicon Investor, The Motley Fool, Yahoo! Finance, and The Raging Bull.

### Silicon Investor

Silicon Investor's Stock Talk (www.techstocks.com) claims to be the largest financial discussion site on the Web, boasting some 300,000 messages a month. It is undoubtedly *the* discussion center for technology stocks.

The format is a message board (Figure 9.5), with thousands of boards organized by technology sectors (computers, software, communications, semiconductors, and Web information). You can use the site search feature to find boards on specific topics or stocks or check out the hottest subjects; then bookmark your favorites. In addition, the Talk section features more than two dozen general investing topics, and the Coffee Shop has more than 100 general topics, from virus alerts to the Starr report.

Silicon Investor is one of the few discussion centers that charges a fee: $100 a year or $200 for a lifetime membership (with a free two-week trial period). You can read messages without charge.

### The Motley Fool

The community center at The Motley Fool (http://boards.fool.com) is clean, crisp, well organized, and very popular (Figure 9.6). There are boards for Stocks A to Z—you can create a new one if your favorite stock is not listed. A Top 25 list points you to the most popular boards.

For a walk on the wacky side, check out the Fools of a Feather. You'll find boards targeted to baby boomers, college kids, retirees, the self-employed, teens, women, and "Left-Handed Fools in Akron."

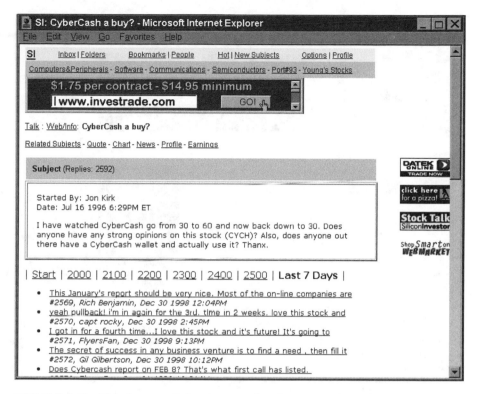

**FIGURE 9.5** This is one of the thousands of message boards at Silicon Investor. (Reprinted with permission of Go2Net, Inc.)

Users can complete a self-profile for viewing by other users, which is standard at most sites, but the Fool adds a clever and typically irreverent touch. You're invited to complete an interview questionnaire (full of Barbara Walter-ish questions) which can be viewed by others and may be featured on the message board home page.

## Yahoo! Finance

Another popular gathering spot is Yahoo! Finance (quote.yahoo.com). It has more than 8000 message boards for stocks alone, organized by industry and a dozen or more investing categories, including brokerages, market trends, and short-term trading.

It also has a freewheeling live chat room called Stock Talk (Figure 9.7), and like most chat rooms, it is chaotic and full of inane postings. We have to admit that some of the inanity may be unintended. We inadvertently clicked on a "cyber-emotion" labeled "kenny." Seconds later we saw a posting with our name, screaming, "They killed kenny, they killed

**FIGURE 9.6** A list of message board categories at The Motley Fool. (Reprinted with permission of The Motley Fool, Inc.)

kenny." (We learned from another poster that kenny is—was?—a character on a television show called *SouthPark*.)

**Chatting at Yahoo!** To get to the stock room at Yahoo! Chat, enter this URL: http://chat.yahoo.com, then click Stock Talk. The name of the main room is Biz: StockWatch.

**Moderated Chats** Yahoo! Chat regularly hosts moderated sessions with market experts from Individual Investor Online, TheStreet.com, and other financial companies. See the Yahoo! Events Calendar on the Yahoo! Chat home page.

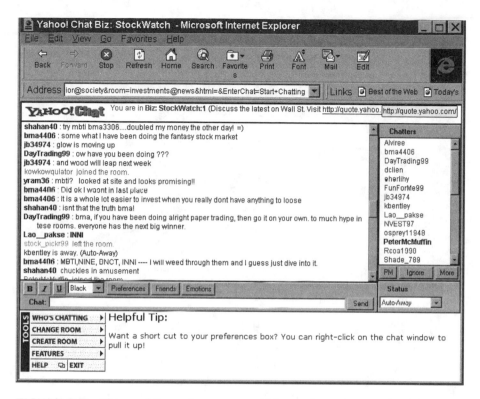

**FIGURE 9.7** This real-time chat room at Yahoo! gives you an idea of the intellectual level of the chat. (Reprinted with permission of Yahoo!)

**Emoticons and Acronyms** Emoticons are a sort of "cyber-shorthand" for expressing emotion in chat groups or e-mail. For example, a colon, a hyphen, and a closing parenthesis :-) indicates happy; switch to an opening parenthesis to indicate sad :-(. Acronyms are a shorthand for common phrases. For example, IMHO means "in my humble opinion." Check out the "dictionaries" at www.chatlist.com and www.randomhouse.com/ features/davebarry/emoticon.html.

## The Raging Bull

The Raging Bull (www.ragingbull.com) was started in 1997 by three college students and is now giving the Big Three a run for their impressions (Figure 9.8). It now boasts 15,000 unique users a day. The site has a

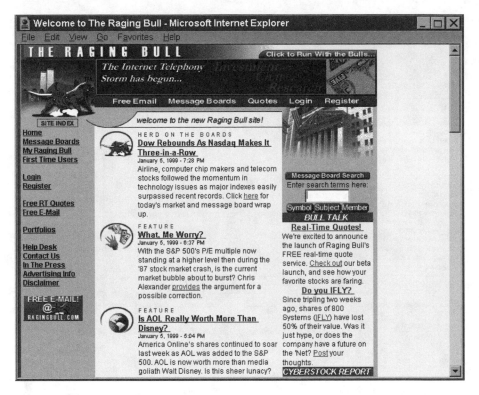

**FIGURE 9.8** The home page of The Raging Bull. (Reprinted with permission of Raging Bull, Inc.)

friendly, well-designed look, with message boards grouped into 13 categories, including the Top 40 most active boards and an OTC bulletin board. You can track your favorite boards and members and—*hallelujah!*—use an IgnoreButton to filter irritating or inane posts.

The Raging Bull makes a valiant attempt to impose a sense of accountability on its members with its Voluntary Disclosure option. Posters are asked to state their position in a stock they're touting or trashing and give it a specific buy/hold/sell rating rather than a torrent of words. (Will they change their name to The Running Bear if the market goes into a major decline?)

## And Consider These . . .

If the Big Four don't meet your chatting and posting appetite, try these:

✔ *The American Association of Individual Investors* (www.aaii.com) sponsors a dozen message boards for everything from investing basics to stocks, brokers, mutual funds, and more. You don't have to be a member to use them, but you do have to register.

✔ *The Armchair Millionaire* (www.armchairmillionaire.com) hosts 25 live chat rooms and 100 message boards, including one on DRIPs and one on employee stock option plans.

✔ *Morningstar.Net's* Conversations include boards on mutual funds, stocks, and more than a dozen general investing forums (www.morningstar.net). Of interest to novice investors is the forum on Investment Basics where you can, in Morningstar's words, "ask any question (no matter how basic), share any idea, and grow as an investor."

✔ *Quicken.com* and *Excite* offer many message boards on investing (boards.excite.com/boards).

✔ *Money.com* (www.money.com) sponsors live moderated chats with market experts on Yahoo! Chat and CompuServe (Figure 9.9). To see a schedule of upcoming chats and archived transcripts, use URL: pathfinder.com/money/chat. The site also has more than 60 message boards (click Bulletin Board at the Money.com home page).

✔ *Special-interest chat rooms* are devoted to specific types of investing.

IPO Intelligence Online (www.ipo-fund.com).

Mutual Funds Interactive (www.fundsinteractive.com).

DripCentral.com (www.dripcentral.com).

401Kafé (www.401kafe.com) Chat about your 401(k).

## The UseNet Newsgroups

The UseNet newsgroups are the original message boards. They number more than 8000 and cover every imaginable subject, including the following boards for investors:

misc.invest.canada.

misc.invest.financial-plan.

misc.invest.futures.

misc.invest.marketplace.

misc.invest.misc.

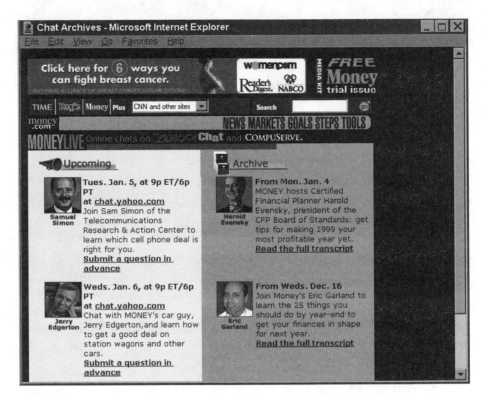

**FIGURE 9.9** These are some of the experts who have appeared on Money.com's moderated chats. Transcripts are available in the archives. (Copyright © 1998 Time Inc. New Media. All rights reserved. Reproduction in whole or in part without permission is prohibited. Pathfinder is a registered trademark of Time Inc. New Media.)

    misc.invest.options.

    misc.invest.stocks (Figure 9.10).

    misc.invest.technical.

    alt.invest.penny-stocks.

    aus.invest (Australia).

Access to newsgroups is controlled by your Internet service provider (ISP) and your browser. First, obtain the name of the news server from your ISP; then configure your browser. On Netscape, enter the information in the Mail and News Preferences on the Options menu. On Internet Explorer, simply select Newsgroups from the menu bar and then follow the prompts.

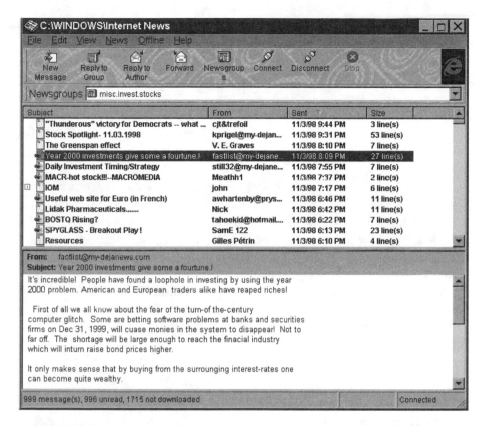

**FIGURE 9.10** The misc.invest.stocks newsgroup is one of the most popular investing newsgroups.

The communities we've described barely scratch the surface of ubiquitous talk centers on the Web. You'll find more boards and chat rooms at the investing magazines (the *e-zines*), online news organizations, and special interest sites like WomensWire (www.womenswire.com), Women's Connection Online (www.womenconnect.com), and iVillage (www.ivillage.com). If chatting's your game, the Internet is a great big gameboard!

 **E-zines** Electronic versions of magazines on the Web; also called 'zines.

To wrap up this chapter of somewhat disparate topics, let us introduce you to banking on the World Wide Web, which is just now beginning to get off the ground.

## BANKING ON THE INTERNET

As it has in so many other areas, the Internet has streamlined the banking process, giving consumers access to bank accounts and electronic bill paying on the Web. It has increased competition among banks as state lines disappear in the seamless realm of cyberspace. It has even spawned virtual banks that have no brick-and-mortar counterparts. What this means for individual investors is a plethora of banking services at their fingertips.

The banking services most streamlined by the Internet are interest rates. Remember when you had to call up your bank to find out its interest rates for a money market account or *certificate of deposit (CD)*? Or phone half a dozen mortgage companies looking for the best mortgage rates? Ditto for auto loans or credit cards or home equity loans.

Not anymore.

Now you can browse a bank's Web site to find its best rates and then compare them with those of one or a dozen other banks. Better yet, check out one of the nonbanking sites whose only raison d'être seems to be to help you find the best interest rates not only locally but across the country.

Let's look at a couple of nonbanking sites. Then we'll tell you where to find some of the top bank sites for online banking.

### Bank Rate Monitor

Bank Rate Monitor (www.bankrate.com) is a big, fat, jam-packed banking portal that has news and articles about personal finance, calculators for figuring out your loan payments, and comparative interest rates on CDs, money market accounts, mortgages, auto loans, credit cards, and home equity loans (Figure 9.11).

**Hable Español**   The Bank Rate Monitor site can be viewed in Spanish.

To stay ahead of the curve, you can sign up for a free e-mail alert for major changes in mortgage, CD, or federal discount rates. A section called The Basics contains how-to guides for managing every aspect of your personal finances, and a feature called Safe & Sound rates the financial condition of more than 10,000 financial institutions.

**FIGURE 9.11** The Bank Rate Monitor offers rates and news on the credit industry. (Source: Bank Rate Monitor, North Palm Beach, FL, copyright © 1998, www.bankrate.com. Reprinted with permission.)

## BanxQuote

You may have seen the BanxQuote logo on some investing supersites. Click the logo and you'll see a page full of pull-down menus that lead to rates and information on auto, home, and consumer finance, as well as money markets, CDs, and government securities. It's the same information that's available at BanxQuote's own Web site at www.banxquote.com (Figure 9.12).

An interesting twist: You can fill out a short form and get an instantaneous quote on a term or annuity life insurance policy.

## And Consider These . . .

Here are some other specialized interest rate sites you may find helpful:

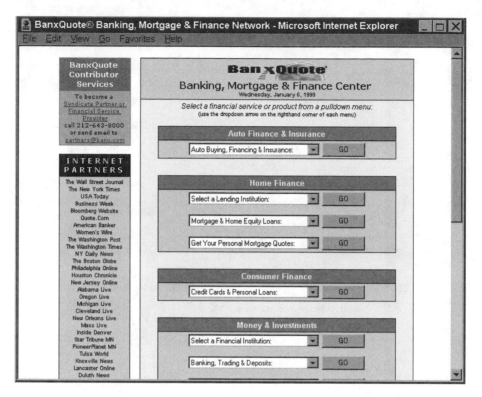

**FIGURE 9.12**  The home page of BanxQuote's Banking, Mortgage & Finance Center. (Reprinted with permission of BanxQuote, Inc.)

✔ CardWeb (www.ramresearch.com) has everything you ever wanted to know about credit cards.

✔ MBNA (www.mbnainternational.com) offers CD and money market rates.

**CD Brokers**  CD brokers are agents licensed to sell securities that specialize in certificates of deposit. Often such brokers can offer CDs with higher yields than CDs purchased directly from a bank. Just make sure the CDs you purchase are insured by the Federal Deposit Insurance Corporation (FDIC).

✔ The Federally Insured Savings Network (www.fisn.com) is a broker for high-yield CDs.

✔ Mortgage Market Information Services (www.interest.com) is a clearinghouse of mortgage information on the Net.

## Online Banking

Online banking has been around for more than a decade, but with the recent merger mania among banks, it has emerged as a prominent, highly touted feature on bank Web sites. What that means to many people—in addition to the convenience of 24-hour banking—is a lot of confusion. How much banking can you do on the Internet? Do you still need banking software? Is it safe?

The short answers are: a lot, probably, and yes.

Some banks have embraced the Internet with a big bear hug. At those sites, online banking includes everything except the physical exchange of greenbacks. You can check balances on the Internet, view account activity on all your accounts, transfer funds between accounts, and handle myriad housekeeping chores such as address changes. On some sites you can also pay bills electronically, although some still require that you use money management software, such as Quicken or Microsoft Money. These are also necessary for generating management or tax reports. Most banks allow you to download your account into these programs.

With regard to safety, the general consensus is that banking over the Web is safe. All bank sites use Secure Sockets Layer (SSL) encryption (the industry standard), which we discussed in Chapter 6. For even tighter security, banks may require 128-bit encryption, which limits your browser choices to Netscape Navigator 4.0 or Microsoft Internet Explorer 4.0. Another safety measure is the user ID and password that are required to access your account.

Let's look now at two banks that are pure products of the Internet.

**The Internet Banks**    NetB@nk and Security First Network Bank (SFNB) both originated on the Internet. And both, interestingly, came from Atlanta. Both offer complete banking services, including money market accounts, CDs, and credit cards. NetB@nk (www.netbank.com) has completely free electronic bill payments (Figure 9.13). SFNB (www.sfnb.com) is free for the first 20 payments, then 20 cents per payment (Figure 9.14).

**Tips for Banking Online**

Here are 10 tips for getting getting started in banking online:

1. ***Try the demo.*** If you've never banked online, test-drive the demo at a bank Web site. (Wells Fargo has a good one—www.wellsfargo.com.) It will give you a feel for what online banking is like before you sign up.

2. ***Understand the online fees.*** Fees for online banking can be complex, so be sure you read the fine print that describes fees for account access versus fees for electronic bill paying versus fees for regular account maintenance. To avoid surprises, tally all the fees before you sign up.

3. ***Get the FAQs.*** The frequently asked questions (FAQ) page may well be the handiest page on the entire bank site. A thorough, well-written FAQ will answer almost any question you have about the bank's fees and electronic bill payment.

4. ***Money talks.*** Many fees can be eliminated if you keep enough funds in your account. Find out if your bank considers total funds in all your accounts in assessing fees. (They should!)

5. ***Don't expect to pay all bills electronically.*** For onetime payments, it may be better to write the check yourself. Most banks will send a bank check to payees who are not part of their system, but you may have to complete a fairly detailed background form about the payee.

6. ***Look for free customer support.*** If a payment goes awry or if you simply have a question, you should be able to reach a real person. Look for an 800 customer service number on the Web site. A missing or hard-to-find number could be indicative of the bank's attitude toward its customers.

7. **Understand regulations for out-of-state banks.** On the Internet you can open an account in another state with ease. However, states differ in their banking regulations, and not every fee or service will apply in every state. This should be spelled out somewhere on the bank Web site, probably in the FAQ.

8. **Don't toss your cookies.** These cookies are bits of data, such as your password and user ID, that are stored on your computer and accessed by the bank for reasons of speed and convenience. Some banks require them, so you may need to set up your browser to accept cookies.

9. **Guard your ID and password.** These should be just as verboten to outside eyes as your secret ATM code. Guard them carefully.

10. **Don't forget to log off!** The Internet might be as secure as Fort Knox, but if you forget to log off after an online session, you're asking for trouble. If you access your account at the office, your financial secrets are open to anyone who walks by. (Don't forget the snooping power of a browser's Back button!) Most banks will automatically log you off after a certain period of inactivity, but the damage could already be done by then.

Other Internet banks are cyber-branches of established banks. If your bank is not yet Internet-ready, you may want to consider one of those listed here:

Bank of America (www.bankamerica.com).

BankBoston (www.bkb.com).

Bank One (www.bankone.com).

Citibank (www.citibank.com).

Dollar Bank (www.dollarbank.com).

First Union National Bank (www.firstunion.com).

Home Savings (www.homesavings.com).

Union Bank of California (www.ucob.com).

U.S. Bank (www.usbank.com).

Wells Fargo (www.wellsfargo.com).

Banking over the Internet is still in its infancy, but it is growing rapidly. Someday, cyber-branches will be as commonplace as neighborhood branches and as easy to use as your ATM card.

**Online Banking Guide**   A comparison of online banking features and fees can be found at www.cyberinvest.com.

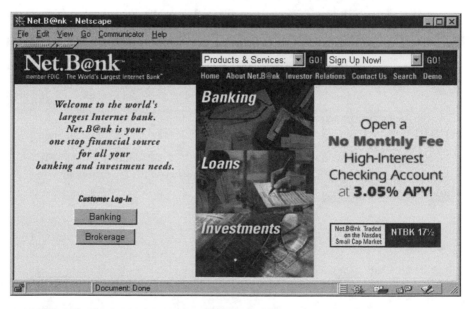

**FIGURE 9.13**   The home page of Net.B@nk, one of two Internet-only banks. (Reprinted with permission of NetB@nk.)

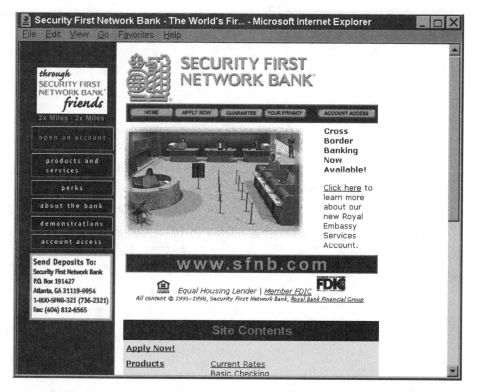

**FIGURE 9.14** The home page of Security First Network Bank, the other Internet-only bank. (Reproduced with permission of Security First Network Bank.)

## SUMMARY

The topics that we've mentioned in this chapter—IPOs, DPOs, DRIPs, DSPs, online communities, and online banking—are all in a state of flux. They've been nurtured and expanded and enhanced by the explosive growth of the Internet over the past few years. As the Internet matures, they and we will continue to feel its effects.

## WEB SITES IN THIS CHAPTER

*IPOs and DPOs*

CBS MarketWatch                cbs.marketwatch.com/news/
                               newsroom.htx

Direct Stock Market            www.directstockmarket.com

| | |
|---|---|
| Emerging Companies Network | www.capital-network.com |
| E*Trade | www.etrade.com |
| Hoover's IPO Central | www.ipocentral.com |
| IPO.com | www.ipo.com |
| IPO Intelligence Online | www.ipo-fund.com |
| IPO Maven | www.ipomaven.com |
| PersonalWealth.com | www.personalwealth.com |
| Quicken.com | quicken.elogic.com/ipo/index.asp |
| Red Herring | www.redherring.com |
| Charles Schwab & Co. | www.eschwab.com |
| Securities and Exchange Commission | www.sec.gov |
| Wit Capital | www.witcapital.com |
| Yahoo! Finance | quote.yahoo.com |
| ZDNet | www.zdnet.com |

### DRIPs, DRPs, DIPs, and DSPs

| | |
|---|---|
| DRIP Central | www.dripcentral.com |
| DRIP Investor | www.dripinvestor.com |
| First Chicago Trust Company | www.fctc.com |
| Kidstock.com | www.kidstock.com |
| The MoneyPaper | www.moneypaper.com |
| The Motley Fool | www.fool.com |
| Netstock Direct | www.netstockdirect.com |
| PersonalWealth.com | www.personalwealth.com |
| Quicken.com | www.quicken.com/investments/drips |
| Stock1.com | www.stock1.com |
| Wall Street Research Net | www.wsrn.com |

### Chat Rooms and Message Boards

| | |
|---|---|
| American Association of Individual Investors | www.aaii.com |

| | |
|---|---|
| Armchair Millionaire | www.armchairmillionaire.com |
| Dave Barry's Emoticons | www.randomhouse.com/features/ davebarry/emoticon.html |
| Dictionary for Chatters | www.chatlist.com |
| DRIP Central | www.dripcentral.com |
| Forbes | www.forbes.com |
| Individual Investor Online | www.iionline.com |
| IPO Intelligence Online | www.ipo-fund.com |
| Ivillage | www.ivillage.com |
| Money.com | www.money.com |
| Morningstar.Net | www.morningstar.net |
| The Motley Fool | http://boards.fool.com |
| Mutual Funds Interactive | www.fundsinteractive.com |
| Quicken.com/Excite | boards.excite.com/boards |
| The Raging Bull | www.ragingbull.com |
| Charles Schwab Investment Center | www.schwab.com |
| Silicon Investor | www.techstocks.com |
| The Wall Street Journal Interactive Edition | www.wsj.com |
| Women's Connection Online | www.womenconnect.com |
| WomensWire | www.womenswire.com |
| Yahoo! Chat | chat.yahoo.com |

*Banks*

| | |
|---|---|
| Bank of America | www.bankamerica.com |
| BankBoston | www.bkb.com |
| Bank One | www.bankone.com |
| Bank Rate Monitor | www.bankrate.com |
| BanxQuote | www.banxquote.com |
| CardWeb | www.ramresearch.com |
| Citibank | www.citibank.com |
| CyberInvest.com | www.cyberinvest.com |
| Dollar Bank | www.dollarbank.com |

| Federally Insured Savings Network | www.fisn.com |
| First Union National Bank | www.firstunion.com |
| Home Savings | www.homesavings.com |
| MBNA | www.mbnainternational.com |
| Mortgage Market Information Services | www.interest.com |
| NetB@nk | www.netbank.com |
| Union Bank of California | www.ucob.com |
| U.S. Bank | www.usbank.com |
| Wells Fargo | www.wellsfargo.com |

# Continuing Education

Investing is a vast subject. It encompasses all the topics touched upon in this book and much, much more. There are, for example, topics that fall under the personal finance umbrella that are rightly considered part of investing, such as IRAs and 401(k)s. To cover all things financial, however, would take a library of books.

The "Getting Started In" series should be part of every beginning investor's library, but online investors have a leg up on their offline counterparts. Virtually everything you want to know about the many facets of investing is available on the Internet, and it's packaged in tasty, bite-sized, usually free pieces. Think of them as educational hors d'oeuvres. Such morsels can satisfy your immediate craving for information, but they won't take the place of the substantial meal offered by a well-written book.

The investing supersites and the speciality sites mentioned in these pages offer a veritable feast of education material. Of particular note are the columns and opinion pieces at the news and investing magazine sites listed in Chapter 5. For specifics on who has what kinds of educational offerings, bookmark the Investing 101 and 102 guides at CyberInvest.com (www.cyberinvest.com), or check out the education sections at InvestorGuide (www.investorguide.com) or FinanceWise (www.finance wise.com).

In fact, these sites and major portal sites, such as Netscape's Netcenter, Microsoft's Start, Yahoo!, Lycos, and Snap.com, can help you stay abreast of the continual changes in the online investing arena. For change it will. Many trends have emerged over the past months, which we expect to grow and consolidate over the next year or two. Among them:

✔ The lowering of price barriers as investing Web sites move premium resources into the free area and lower prices in general.

✔ A pay-per-report system rather than site subscriptions, for such things as company profiles, earnings estimates, and search reports.

✔ Web sites transforming into "hubs" that give investors more reasons to stick around or return, and yet provide gateways to other Web resources.

✔ The blurring of lines between discount and full service brokers resulting in a new cyber-entity, the Web broker.

✔ Customization of Web pages, which lets you pick and choose what you want to see and do on a site.

✔ Intelligent reports that explain each item as you move through the report.

✔ More powerful search programs, more precise alert systems, more globalization, more and more of more and more.

The problem, of course, is the "more and more." Among the most welcome trends are tools like customization and intelligent reports that attempt to guide you through the deluge of data, rather than merely adding to it. As an online investor, you will be in the first wave of those to benefit from these trends. Our advice is to start now and get the learning curve out of the way.

# Glossary

**administrative fee**  a charge assessed by the management company to maintain your mutual fund account.

**Adobe Acrobat Reader**  a free, downloadable software program that allows you to view, navigate, and print PDF files across all major computing platforms. Available at www.adobe.com.

**aftermarket performance**  the performance of an IPO after it has begun trading, usually in comparison with the offering price.

**alert**  a notification (by e-mail, pager, or portfolio flag) of an event relating to a stock or mutual fund. Events can be a price increase or decrease, news about the stock, earnings announcements, or a significant change in the stock's trading patterns.

**all or none (AON)**  a buy or sell order that specifies that unless the entire order can be filled, the order should be canceled.

**American Depositary Receipt (ADR)**  a receipt given a foreign-based corporation for shares it places in the vault of a U.S. bank for selling to investors. An ADR entitles the non-U.S. company to have a listing on a U.S. exchange. Instead of buying shares in the foreign corporation, American investors can buy shares in the U.S.-based ADR.

**analyst**  an individual employed by a brokerage house or institutional investor to research a specific industry and the companies in that industry and write research reports on the future growth potential of both. Also called industry analysts, research analysts, and Wall Street analysts.

**asset allocation**  the process of dividing your investment dollars among various classes of financial assets.

**asset class**  a major category of investments, such as cash, stocks, and bonds. Subclasses for stocks are domestic stocks and international stocks; subclasses for bonds are Treasuries, municipal bonds, and corporate bonds; subclasses of cash are money market accounts and certificates of deposit.

**back-end load**   the sales commission on mutual fund transactions that is charged at the time of redemption or sale, rather than at the time of purchase. The latter is a front-end load.

**back-testing**   Telescan back-tests searches by running the search on the first day of each month for the past 12 months and plotting the performance of the top 25 stocks from each search to the current day. (The back-testing chart slopes from left to right because the more recent stocks have had less time to perform.) The objective is to find searches that perform well consistently.

**bank-sponsored plans**   a direct stock purchase plan (DSP) or dividend reinvestment plan (DRIP) that is administered by a bank rather than the company itself.

**basing**   a technical trading pattern that occurs when the distance lessens between a stock's support and resistance levels and the stock trades within a very narrow price range for a period of time.

**bear market**   a period in which market prices tend to fall and the commonly reported market indexes, such as the NASDAQ OTC index and the S&P 500, are below their 200-day moving average.

**Bloomberg terminal**   the computer terminal used by stockbrokers and other professional investors, which is fed by a 24-hour, real-time news and financial information stream from Bloomberg.

**blue chips**   stocks of large, well-known companies that have a long record of growth and dividend payments. The 30 stocks that make up the Dow Jones Industrial Average are blue-chip stocks, but not the only blue-chip stocks.

**Bollinger bands**   a variation on trading bands created by John Bollinger, in which the envelope is plotted at standard deviation levels above and below the moving average, which allows the bands to self-adjust to the volatility of the market (they widen during periods of volatility and contract during periods of calm).

**bond**   a bond is a security representing debt, as opposed to a security representing ownership or equity (stocks). With a debt security, you are in effect lending money to the entity that issues the bond—the federal, state, or local government, corporations, mortgage companies, and so on—and receiving a fixed interest rate on your loan.

**bond swaps**   a municipal bond investment strategy that lets you take a tax loss and adjust your bond portfolio for credit quality and maturities to meet market considerations and your personal needs. Also called tax swap.

**bookmark** saving the URL of a Web site in a special browser folder for easy access in the future. (On Internet Explorer it is called Favorites on the menu bar; on Netscape Navigator it is called Bookmarks.)

**breakout** a change in a technical indicator that generates a change in the trading signal, from a hold to a buy or sell, from a buy to a sell, or from a sell to a buy.

**browser** software that allows you to view documents on the World Wide Web. The two major browsers are Netscape Navigator and Microsoft Internet Explorer.

**bull market** a period in which market prices tend to rise and the commonly reported market indexes, such as the NASDAQ OTC index and the S&P 500, are above their 200-day moving average.

**cache** a folder on your computer for temporary storage of Internet files. This allows the browser to quickly retrieve a Web page that has been previously viewed. To retrieve a new version of a page stored in your cache, click your browser's Refresh or Reload button.

**call** an option contract that gives the holder the right to buy the underlying security at a specific price for a specific period of time. Calls can be bought or sold.

**cash flow** a company's net income with adjustments for noncash items. For example, a noncash expense such as depreciation would be added back to net income to arrive at cash flow.

**certificate of deposit (CD)** an insured, fixed-term, interest-bearing debt investment issued by a bank that pays a fixed rate of interest over the specific period of time, with penalties for early withdrawal.

**chat room** an area of a Web site that allows users to communicate with other users in real time by typing messages that appear on the screen to be viewed by anyone who is in that particular chat room.

**climbing the band** a pattern that occurs in trading bands or Bollinger bands when a stock trades near the upper band for a period of time.

**cobranded page** a page at a Web site that is cosponsored by another Web site.

**contrarian strategy** an investing strategy that appears to go against the mood of the market, buying heavily during sluggish, pessimistic markets and selling during periods of market optimism.

**corporate bonds**   debt obligations issued by private and public corporations; compare with shares of stocks issued by corporations, which are equity instruments.

**corporate insider**   an officer or director of a public company or a major shareholder who owns more than 10 percent of a company's shares. These shareholders must file a disclosure report with the SEC anytime they buy or sell shares of the company stock.

**country fund**   a closed-end mutual fund which invests its assets in the securities of companies within a given country (e.g., the Thailand Fund).

**covered call**   a call option written by a person who owns the underlying security.

**criteria**   in stock screening, the factors that describe the characteristics of a stock you are seeking. For example, the criteria for finding undervalued growth stocks would be low P/E ratio and high earnings growth. Only stocks that exhibit those characteristics will pass the screen.

**currency conversion**   the converting of one country's currency into the currency of another country. Most international Web sites offer currency conversion tables.

**day order**   an order to buy or sell a security that expires at the end of the day.

**day trading**   the practice of basing trades on market fluctuations during the day and closing out positions by the end of the trading day.

**delayed quotes**   stock quotes that are delayed by the exchanges 15 or 20 minutes from real-time.

**derivative security**   a security whose value is based on (derived from) another (underlying) security, such a stock or market index. Options and futures are derivatives.

**DIP**   *see* **direct investment plan.**

**direct enrollment**   a dividend reinvestment plan that allows an individual to purchase stock directly from the company.

**direct investment plan (DIP)**   allows an individual to buy shares directly from a company. Also called a direct stock purchase plan (DSP).

**direct public offering (DPO)**   an initial public offering that bypasses the traditional underwriter and offers shares directly to the public over the Internet. Also called an online stock offering.

**direct stock plan (DSP)**   *see* **direct investment plan (DIP).**

**dividend reinvestment plan (DRIP)**  this plan automatically purchases a company's stock with a shareholder's dividends from that stock.

**dividend yield**  the annual dividends from a stock divided by the current stock price.

**dollar-cost averaging**  a system of investing a fixed sum at regular intervals in stocks or mutual funds. Acquiring more shares at lower prices and fewer shares at higher prices helps minimize your market risk.

**Dow dividend approach**  an investing strategy that invests equally in the 10 stocks of the Dow 30 that pay the highest dividends.

**Dow Jones Industrial Average (the Dow)**  the best-known U.S. stock index, which is made up of 30 of the largest U.S. companies. It is a barometer of market activity.

**download**  the process of transferring files from the Web onto your hard drive.

**DRIP**  *see* **dividend reinvestment plan.**

**drop-down menu**  a small window on a Web page that "drops down" a list of multiple options when the down-arrow is clicked. Also called a pull-down menu.

**DRP**  *see* **DRIP.**

**DSP**  *see* **DIP.**

**due diligence**  the process of checking a company's background and financial condition in order to deem it worthy of offering its shares to the public in an initial public offering.

**earnings per share (EPS)**  a company's total earnings (profits) divided by the number of outstanding shares of stock.

**earnings surprises**  a positive earnings surprise occurs when a company exceeds the analysts' projected estimates of its quarterly or annual earnings per share. A negative surprise occurs when the company fails to meet the analysts' expectations.

**EDGAR**  an acronym for the SEC's paperless filing system for public companies. It stands for Electronic Data Gathering, Analysis and Retrieval. EDGAR filings include 10Ks and 10Qs, but the SEC reports that 95 percent of all insider transactions are still filed in paper form.

**emerging growth stocks**  stocks of companies that are in growth industries but which have not yet begun to show earnings. Examples would be a biotech company that has products in the pipeline but has not yet received the required government approval or an Internet stock whose earnings have not yet materialized.

**European Monetary Union (EMU)**   refers to the single monetary and economic policy within Europe that established the European Central Bank and creates and controls the common currency—the euro.

**exchange fee**   fee charged by a mutual fund family for exchanging shares of one fund for shares of another. Also, fee charged by a stock exchange for dissemination of stock quotes.

**expiration date**   the date on which the right to exercise a particular option expires.

**expiration month codes**   the month in which the right to exercise a particular option expires; each month has a code which becomes part of the ticker symbol for that option.

**exponential moving average**   a moving average smooths the fluctuations in stock prices by averaging the prices over a specified period. An exponential moving average gives heavier weight to the most recent data.

**e-zines**   electronic versions of magazines on the Web; also called 'zines.

**federal agency securities**   debt securities issued by Fannie Mae, Freddie Mac, Sallie Mae, Connie Lee, and others—otherwise known as, respectively, the Federal National Mortgage Association, the Federal Home Loan Mortgage Corporation, the Student Loan Marketing Association, the College Construction Loan Insurance Association, and others.

**fill or kill**   a buy order that instructs the broker to complete the trade by the end of the current trading day or cancel it.

**financial ratios**   comparisons of market price, balance sheet items, and income statement items, such as debt-to-equity, price-to-earnings, or price-to-book value.

**foreign exchange rate**   the ratio of one country's currency to another country's currency.

**foreign government bonds**   bonds issued and backed by the reputation and good faith of foreign governments.

**front-end load**   the sales commission on mutual fund transactions that is charged at the time of purchase, rather than at the time of redemption. The latter is a back-end load.

**fundamental analysis** evaluating a stock by assessing a company's intrinsic worth and growth potential based on such factors as historical earnings, projected earnings, revenues, cash flow, and various financial ratios.

**fundamentals** factors that contribute to a company's basic financial health, such as earnings, revenues, cash flow, debt level, and financial ratios.

**futures contract** a contract that allows an investor to buy or sell a commodity, such as oil, wheat, or gold, at some time in the future.

**good till canceled (GTC)** an order to buy or sell a security that is good until it is either filled or canceled.

**government securities** debt instruments such as Treasury bills, Treasury bonds, or Treasury notes that are issued by the U.S. government.

**greenshoe** in an IPO, this is a percentage of the total underwriting, usually 15 percent, that can be purchased by the underwriters in addition to the scheduled allotment of shares. The greenshoe is usually invoked if the deal is hot or overbooked. It is also called an overallotment.

**hard stop** a stop order issued to a broker to sell a stock should it reach a specified price.

**high techs** stocks that are based on technology, such as computer-related stocks or Internet stocks.

**historical earnings** a company's earnings per share over a past period.

**hyperlink** consists of a text or a graphic item that contains an HTML code that causes another page within the Web site or a completely different Web site to be retrieved and displayed. Text links are usually underlined and shown in a different color from surrounding text. A mouse cursor changes shape when placed over a text or graphic link.

**industry group** an index of stocks in the same industry. Industry groups were created as a method of tracking the performance of a similar group of stocks.

**industry group rotation** the process of industry groups moving into and out of favor with institutional investors, based on some economic event, real or imagined.

**initial public offering (IPO)** a company's first offering of stock to the public, usually to be traded over one of the exchanges; also known as "going public."

**in play** refers to a stock that is known to be a candidate for a takeover or merger, which often throws it into a public bidding contest between two or more suitors.

**in registration**   in an IPO, the period that starts at time a company files its registration statement with the SEC and continues for 25 days, during which a company is restricted from promoting the offering in any way. Also called the quiet period.

**insider trading**   the buying and selling of stock by corporate insiders.

**institutional investor**   a mutual fund, pension fund, or other investment firm managed by a professional money manager.

**Internet service provider (ISP)**   a company that provides software and communications links to the Internet. Two of the larger ISPs are Netcom and AT&T, but there are hundreds of smaller ISPs.

**intraday chart**   a price-and-volume stock chart that tracks the minute-by-minute trades during the day.

**investment objective**   the stated financial goal of a mutual fund, which serves to identify the types of investments sought by the fund.

**Java**   a computer language designed by Sun Microsystems that uses moving text, animation, and interactivity. Some older browsers are not "Java-enabled."

**leading economic indicators**   statistical reports issued by the U.S. government that indicate the condition of the economy. Some leading economic indicators are unemployment, productivity, housing starts, disposable personal income, gross domestic product, retail sales, and the consumer price index.

**limit order**   an order to buy or sell securities at a specific price or better.

**listed stock**   stock that is listed on the New York Stock Exchange or American Stock Exchange. Technically, NASDAQ stocks are traded over the counter and are not considered listed stocks.

**load**   the sales commission charged by mutual funds on share transactions. A front-end load is a commission charged on purchases; a back-end load is a commission charged on redemptions.

**lock-up period**   the time period after an initial public offering when the insiders are prohibited from selling their shares. The lock-up period usually lasts 180 days.

**long**   refers to securities owned by an investor and held in the investor's brokerage account.

**LSQ line**   LSQ stands for a mathematical formula called "least squares." In technical analysis, an LSQ line is a trend line that determines the midpoint of price data on a stock graph. An LSQ channel is created by drawing parallel lines on either side of the LSQ line to encompass the trading action.

**management fee**   the fee charged by a mutual fund and paid to the mutual fund manager for managing the fund's portfolio.

**margin account**   a brokerage account that allows investors to borrow money against their securities held by that broker.

**market capitalization**   a measure of the size of a company by multiplying the outstanding shares by the price per share; also called market cap.

**market correction**   a relatively short-term reversal of stock prices in an overbought market, which brings the market back to more reasonable values.

**market index**   a grouping of stocks with specific characteristics that is created for the purpose of tracking the performance of the group. For example, the Dow Jones Industrial Average tracks the performance of 30 of the largest U.S. stocks; the ISDEX tracks 50 of the most influential Internet stocks. Some indexes are weighted for capitalization, which favors the large-cap stocks in the index. Unweighted indexes use the simple average of all the stocks in the index.

**market maker**   a firm that "makes a market" in an over-the-counter (NASDAQ) security by maintaining a firm bid and offer price.

**market order**   an order to buy or sell a specified number of shares at the best available price.

**market share**   the percentage of a specific market segment that is dominated or controlled by a player in that market. In the online brokerage market segment, for example, 27.4 percent of all online investors are customers of Charles Schwab & Co., while only 3.3 percent are customers of Discover Brokerage (as of the fourth quarter, 1998).

**market stats**   intraday and closing prices of various market indexes, including the Dow, the NASDAQ, the New York Stock Exchange index, and the S&P 500.

**market top**   a point at which a long-term uptrend reverses and the market heads downward.

**mental stop**   a reminder to reevaluate a stock if it falls to a specified level. The reminder can be a visual flag in an online portfolio or an e-mail message from the Web site that maintains the portfolio.

**message board**   a computerized version of a bulletin board that allows users to communicate with other users on a variety of topics by posting questions, answers, comments, or suggestions. Messages are usually threaded (i.e., responses to a specific message are attached to the original message).

**moderated session** a chat room or message board that features a guest "speaker" who takes questions from users. Such sessions are controlled or moderated by a host who interacts with the guest and screens questions from participants.

**momentum** the strength behind an upward or downward movement in stock price.

**mortgage- and asset-backed securities** securities that hold mortgages or other assets, such as buildings, real estate, or corporate notes.

**moving average** the average of a stock price over a specific time period. A moving average smooths price and volume fluctuations and emphasizes the direction of a trend. An exponential moving average gives greater weight to the most recent price action.

**moving average convergence/divergence (MACD)** a trading method based on the crossing of two exponential moving averages above and below a zero line. (A third moving average plots the difference between the other two and forms a signal line.) The convergence and divergence of the moving averages generate buy and sell signals.

**municipal bond** a bond issued by a state or local government to finance operations or a special project. The income from municipal bonds is exempt from federal income taxes and from taxes by the issuer.

**mutual fund family** a group of mutual funds sponsored or managed by the same investment company. The funds in a family usually span a wide spectrum of investment objectives, which allows investors to diversify their portfolios (by switching money among the funds) without leaving the family.

**National Association of Securities Dealers (NASD)** the parent company of NASDAQ and NASD Regulation, Inc., which is the regulatory body of the over-the-counter securities markets.

**net asset value (NAV)** the price paid for a mutual fund share. The NAV is computed daily by summing the values of all the fund's investments, subtracting expenses and liabilities, and dividing that number by the number of outstanding shares.

**netiquette** the unofficial standards that govern group behavior on the Internet. Some chat rooms and message boards post specific rules that must be observed; some netiquette is learned by observation or trial and error.

**netizens**   people who frequent the Internet.

**newbie**   a new user of the Internet. A cyber rookie, so to speak.

**no-load**   the absence of sales commissions, as in no-load mutual funds.

**OEX**   a commonly traded index option based on the S&P 100.

**offering price**   the price set by the underwriters for shares in an initial public offering, deemed to be a fair market price. Investors allocated shares in the IPO receive the offering price; this is not the same as the opening price, which is the price at which the stock starts trading in the open market.

**online offering**   an initial public offering that takes place on the Internet without the help of a traditional underwriter.

**opening price**   the price at which an IPO stock starts trading on the day it goes public; also called the "first trade price."

**operators**   symbols, such as < (less than) or > (greater than), which are used in some screening programs to qualify the factors used in the screen.

**option**   a contract that gives the holder the right but not the obligation to buy or sell a specified quantity of a security at a specified price within a specified time period.

**option chain**   a list of all tradable options on a given stock.

**order flow**   the buy and sell orders that brokers send to market makers, often in return for cash payments.

**out-of-the-money**   refers to an option whose strike price is greater (if it is a call) or less (if it is a put) than the current market price of the underlying security.

**overbought**   a condition that occurs in the market when there are more buyers than sellers and stock prices hover at a precariously high level. An overbought market is ripe for a correction.

**oversold**   a condition that occurs in the market when there are more sellers than buyers and stock prices fall to extremely low levels. An oversold market is a poised for an upward movement.

**page impression**   one visit to one page on a Web site. Web traffic is measured by the number of page impressions generated by a site.

**partial fill**   a limit order that is only partially filled because the total specified shares could not be bought or sold at the specified price.

**penny stocks**   over-the-counter stocks that trade for (usually) less than $3/share. Quotes are entered by dealers who act as market makers and are printed on "Pink Sheets" (hence the name) by the National Quotation Bureau.

**portal**   a Web site that attempts to be a gateway to other Web sites in specific categories.

**portfolio tracker**   a mechanism on the Web that can retrieve stock prices and other data for multiple securities, allowing you to track the performance and valuation of a portfolio of stocks.

**price-to-book ratio**   a company's stock price divided by its book value.

**price-to-earnings ratio (P/E ratio)**   a company's stock price divided by its annual earnings per share.

**price-to-sales ratio**   a company's stock price divided by its annual sales.

**private key**   a method of decrypting or decoding data received by the server over a secure connection, the data having been encrypted by the user with a public key. Both keys are issued by the server, as part of the Secure Sockets Layer (SSL) protocol.

**profile**   an overview of a company or mutual fund which presents important facts about the company or fund's history, management, financial condition, growth potential, and other pertinent details.

**projected earnings**   a company's expected earnings for the next quarter or next fiscal year as estimated by industry analysts.

**projected five-year growth rate**   the rate at which a company is expected to grow based on its projected earnings by industry analysts.

**prospectus**   a written offer to sell securities, which is filed with the SEC by companies undergoing an initial public offering or a secondary offering or by mutual fund companies. The prospectus sets forth the plan for the proposed business enterprise (in an IPO) or the facts concerning an existing company that an investor needs in order to make an informed decision. Strict rules govern the information that must be disclosed to investors in the prospectus.

**public key**   a method of encrypting or encoding data over a secure connection that is used by the public (the user); the data is then decrypted by the server using a private key. Both keys are issued by the server, as part of the Secure Sockets Layer (SSL) protocol.

**public venture capital offering**   another name for a direct public offering.

**pull-down menu**   *see* **drop-down menu.**

**put** an option contract that gives the holder the right to sell the underlying security at a specific price for a specific period of time. Puts can be bought or sold.

**quarter-over-quarter earnings** a comparison of a company's current quarterly earnings per share with its earnings per share for the same quarter last year.

**quiet period** in an IPO, the period of time during which a company is not allowed to promote its stock or say anything that has not been disclosed in the prospectus. The quiet period starts with the filing of the S-1 registration statement and continues until 25 days after the stock starts trading.

**RealAudio** downloadable software that improves the sound quality on your computer and enables you to enjoy the audio features of many Web sites; available at www.realaudio.com.

**real-time quotes** stock quotes that include the most recent trade, as opposed to quotes that are delayed 15 or 20 minutes by the exchanges. Real-time, continuous live quotes, offered by some Web sites, are real-time quotes that are automatically updated with each new tick of the stock.

**redemption fee** a fee charged by some mutual funds when an investor sells shares in the fund. Also called a back-end load.

**red herring** nickname for the preliminary prospectus filed in an initial public offering, so called because of the warning, printed in red, that the information in the document is incomplete or subject to change.

**registered shareholder** the name in which shares of stock are held in the records of the company's official registrar.

**research alert** an announcement by an industry analyst of either a revision in his or her estimated earnings for a company or an upgrade or downgrade in the buy/sell/hold recommendation.

**research report** a report on a company or industry written by an industry analyst who studies and analyzes the industry and companies within it.

**resistance** a price level that represents a barrier for continued upward movement because in the past the stock price has stopped rising at this level and either moved sideways or reversed direction. Strong momentum is needed to push the stock through a strong resistance level.

**screen** one or more characteristics that are used as a filter to eliminate stocks that don't have those characteristics.

**search engine** a mechanism for finding information, documents, or Web sites on the Internet. The major Web-wide search engine sites are Yahoo!, Lycos, Excite, Alta Vista, InfoSeek, WebCrawler, Snap, Northern Light, and HotBot. Most large Web sites have their own site search engines that search for information within the site.

**SEC filings** 10Ks, 10Qs, and other reports filed by public companies with the Securities and Exchange Commission.

**secondary market** a market in which an investor purchases shares of stocks or other securities from another investor, rather than from the corporation itself. The New York Stock Exchange and NASDAQ are secondary markets. One of the problems with DPOs is there is no readily accessible secondary market.

**sector** a distinct part of the economy, such as the housing sector or the health care sector. Sectors are comprised of related industry groups.

**Secure Sockets Layer (SSL)** this is an encryption/decryption method (the industry standard) that creates a secure channel on the Internet for sending and receiving data. SSL utilizes dual key encryption, with a public key given to users and a private key retained by the server.

**Securities and Exchange Commission (SEC)** the U.S. government agency that regulates public companies.

**Securities Investor Protection Corporation (SIPC)** the SIPC insures brokerage accounts for up to $500,000, of which no more than $100,000 covers cash awaiting reinvestment. The additional coverage offered by many brokerages is supplied by other insurers, such as Lloyds of London.

**selling syndicate** a group of investment banks put together by the lead underwriter to buy shares in an IPO and sell them to the public.

**short interest** the number of a company's shares that have been sold short and not yet repurchased, frequently reported as the number of days it would take to cover the short position, assuming the volume of stock stays at its average volume traded over the past 30 days.

**short selling** selling a security you don't own (borrowed from your broker) with the intention of buying it at a lower price to replace the borrowed shares. Short sellers are betting the price will go down.

**S-1 registration statement** the document filed with the SEC which announces a company's intent to go public. It can be downloaded free at www.sec.gov.

**spread** the gap between the bid and ask prices of a security.

**standard deviation** a statistical measure of volatility.

**STARS ranking system** a one-to-five star ranking system for stocks used by Standard & Poor's based on its assessment of the stock's potential for price growth. Stocks given five stars are expected to be the best short-term performers (within six months to a year). The acronym stands for Stock Appreciation Ranking System.

**stop-limit order** a variation on the stop order; a stop-limit order will be executed only at the limit price, not higher or lower than the limit price. In contrast, a stop order will be executed at the stop price, or, should the stock gap up or down, at the higher- or lower-than-stop price.

**stop order** an order placed at a price that is higher (a buy stop) or lower (a sell stop) than the current market price. Buy stops are used by short sellers; sell stops are employed by investors who trade long. Both are used to protect profits and limit losses.

**Strategic Indexing** the use of an investing strategy that has been back-tested over a long period of time and has exceeded a target index, such as the S&P 500.

**street name** refers to the registered holder of a security when it is held in the broker's name, rather than in the name of the person who owns the stock.

**support** a price level that represents a floor for falling stock prices. It is a price at which buying has historically entered, thereby tending to limit declines below this level.

**technical analysis** evaluating the price potential of a security by studying price-and-volume patterns, using any of dozens of technical indicators.

**ten-bagger** a stock that has a tenfold increase in price.

**10K** the annual report filed by public companies with the SEC, which provides a comprehensive overview of the company. The report must be filed within 90 days after the end of the company's fiscal year.

**10Q** a quarterly report filed by public companies with the SEC which contains unaudited financial statements. The 10Q must be filed within 45 days of the close of first, second, and third quarters of the company's fiscal year.

**thread** a specific topic of "conversation" in a message board, composed of the original message on that topic and all subsequent comments, questions, and answers that relate to that topic.

**tick** an incremental change of a stock price. An uptick means the trade was higher than the one before; a downtick means the trade was lower than the previous trade.

**trading bands**   on a stock graph, an envelope drawn within a set distance on either side of a moving average to delineate a stock's trading range.

**Treasury auctions**   regularly scheduled public auctions held by the U.S. Department of the Treasury which allow you to buy T-bills, T-bonds, and T-notes directly from the government (if you have a Treasury Direct account, which you can set up through your local Federal Reserve Bank). Check the Treasury Department's Web site for the schedule (www.treas.gov/domfin/auction.htm).

**Treasury bills (T-bills)**   a U.S. government debt security that matures in one year or less and is issued for a minimum of $10,000.

**Treasury bonds (T-bonds)**   a U.S. government debt security that matures in 10 to 30 years and is issued in denominations of $1000. The 30-year bond is the bellwether for interest rates.

**Treasury notes (T-notes)**   a U.S. government debt security that matures in 2 to 10 years and is issued in denominations of $1000.

**trend break**   the movement of the stock price through a trend line. A positive trend break is a move upward through a downward trend line; a negative trend break is a move downward through an upward trend line.

**trend line**   a line on a stock graph that connects a series of highs or lows to delineate an uptrend (representing support) or a downtrend (representing resistance).

**12b-1 fee**   a fee deducted from a mutual fund's earnings to cover the fund's sales and marketing expenses.

**underlying security**   the stock, bond, index, or other financial instrument upon which a derivative such as an option is based. It is the underlying security that is subject to being bought or sold upon exercise of the option.

**underwriter**   called the lead underwriter, this is the investment bank that "takes a company public," performing the due diligence, setting the offering price, putting together the selling syndicate, and generally shepherding the company through the many steps of an initial public offering.

**upgrades/downgrades**   analysts make buy/hold/sell recommendations for the stocks they follow. An upgrade is a change from a sell to a hold or buy, or from a hold to a buy. A downgrade is a change from a buy to a hold or sell, or from a hold to a sell.

**URL (Uniform Resource Locator)**   the address of a Web site. The primary URL for a Web site contains the prefix http:// and sometimes, but not always, www (which stands for World Wide Web); then the domain name, which is the actual address of the Web site. For example, CyberInvest.com's domain name is cyberinvest.com. Its entire URL is http://www.cyberinvest.com. In this book, we've omitted the http:// because the newest browsers automatically add this prefix.

**watch list**   a list or portfolio of stock prospects that you are watching with an eye for an optimum entry point.

**whipsaws**   very frequent reversals of a stock between buy and sell signals, based on various technical indicators; also called chatter.

**whisper numbers**   figures widely believed by "those in the know" on Wall Street to be the true earnings that a company will achieve in the next quarter. The whisper numbers often exceed the earnings estimates published by analysts. When a company announces earnings that meet or even exceed the analysts' estimates but fail to meet the whisper numbers, the stock price will often drop.

**yield**   income received from an investment (interest or dividends), divided by the price of the investment. Yield does not include capital gains or losses.

# Index

247